Praise for *Coming*

'Trumpers is irrepressibly naughty, permanently
mischievous and hasn't finished yet . . . But this memoir
isn't just a fascinating, frequently hilarious insight into
the life of a force of nature. It is also, despite itself, an
examination of a particular generation of women, trained
for not much except marriage and cocktail parties,
and of how, given the right spirit, some of those
women derailed in the best possible way and
went on to have wonderful adventures'
India Knight, *Sunday Times*

'Colourful, life-affirming, gloriously funny'
Sunday Express

'Heaven, and everyone who opens it will
fall in love with her'
Rachel Cooke, *Observer*

'On several occasions when I was reading
Baroness Trumpington's autobiography, I had the
disconcerting experience that she was sitting next to me,
speaking directly into my ear, and periodically jabbing
an elbow into my ribs . . . Exuberant,
engaging and very funny'
Daily Mail

Coming Up Trumps

JEAN TRUMPINGTON was born Jean Alys Campbell-Harris in 1922, the daughter of an officer in the Bengal Lancers, and an American heiress. Educated privately, she left school aged fifteen having never taken an exam. With the outbreak of the Second World War, she became first a land girl and then worked in naval intelligence at Bletchley Park. After the war, she moved to New York, where she met her husband, William Barker. They returned to Britain and married in 1954.

Jean Barker, as she then was, began her political career as a Cambridge City Councillor, rising to become Mayor of Cambridge in 1971. She has served in two Conservative governments and in 1980 was made a life peer. She remains an active member of the government front bench and, in November 2012, aged ninety, was the oldest-ever guest to have appeared on *Have I Got News for You*. Widowed in 1988, Baroness Trumpington lives in Battersea.

Jean Trumpington

Coming Up Trumps

A MEMOIR

PAN BOOKS

First published 2014 by Macmillan

First published in paperback 2015 by Pan Books
an imprint of Pan Macmillan, a division of Macmillan Publishers Limited
Pan Macmillan, 20 New Wharf Road, London N1 9RR
Basingstoke and Oxford
Associated companies throughout the world
www.panmacmillan.com

ISBN 978-1-4472-5678-6

135798642

A CIP catalogue record for this book is available from the British Library.

Typeset by Ellipsis Digital Limited, Glasgow
Printed and bound by CPI Group (UK) Ltd, Croydon, CR0 4YY

Visit www.panmacmillan.com to read more about all our books
and to buy them. You will also find features, author interviews and
news of any author events, and you can sign up for e-newsletters
so that you're always first to hear about our new releases.

Contents

Foreword and Acknowledgements

A few months ago, I was doing my weekly shop in Waitrose, and a rather beautiful, rather elegant, little white-haired lady kept bumping into me, and I kept bumping into her. Eventually, I said, 'Look here, my name is Baroness Trumpington, and I am blind and I can't see you and I was at Bletchley.' The little white-haired lady, who was wearing a pink trouser suit and a string of pearls, said, 'I am Princess Radziwill and I worked at Baker Street.' 'Lor!' I said. 'That's very posh.' I knew exactly what Baker Street was: that was the Secret Operations Executive, where all the 007s were briefed before they were sent off to France during the war. 'I'm eighty-nine,' said the Princess. 'I'm ninety,' said I. And we two ancient ladies, who had never met before, congratulated each other on our war effort, and on the coincidence of our meeting in Waitrose in Knightsbridge, and on our still being alive.

I was thrilled, and charmed. But the truth is, this kind of thing happens to me all the time. I have had the most extraordinary life, full of kindness, and incredible good luck, and naughtiness and jolly good fun.

I have met David Lloyd George, Max Beaverbrook, Jackie Kennedy, Bette Davis, Senator McCarthy, Stanley Spencer. Come to think of it, I have in fact met every single post-war prime minister, from Clement Attlee (who I met at the theatre) to David Cameron, and practically every world leader from Her Majesty the Queen to the Assads, Fidel Castro and Robert Mugabe. I was in Manhattan in the fifties, at Cliveden in the sixties, and on Concorde's first and last flights. I seem to have stumbled into fascinating events without really trying, and to have met formidable and extraordinarily interesting people, despite being rather dull myself.

That's one piece of luck. I have also been lucky in my family life. Without a doubt the happiest years of my life were the years I lived with my husband Alan, always known as Barker, and our son Adam at The Leys School in Cambridge. I don't think anybody could have been happier.

I also feel enormously lucky to have had such terribly interesting jobs, despite having never taken an exam in my life – not even a driving test. (I learnt to drive during the war, when we were all given licences without having to take a test.) It started with Bletchley, and my post-war job in Paris, which were both marvellous in their own way. Many years later it was largely through luck that I became a councillor in Cambridge.

My final piece of luck has been finding a second life, and a second family, in the House of Lords. I adored being a minister and learning about this country. I feel honoured to be part of the very special, kind and fun-loving institution that is the House of Lords.

Some would say that people make their own luck. I don't agree. I believe more in fate. Some say that fortune favours the well-prepared. Well, I certainly wasn't well-prepared. There has been no design to my life at all: no plot, no plan. I've lived by the skin of my teeth and taking chances at village dances.

In some ways though, I suppose I have made a small contribution to my good luck.

I have been brave: going to Paris at fifteen, Bletchley at eighteen and New York at twenty-nine, each time on my own and knowing no one; learning to ski, and water ski and goodness knows what else, just to impress a man I was keen on; daring to mix with very grand people on a shoestring; and being prepared to ask for things that others wouldn't have dreamed of mentioning. I was often frightened, but I did it anyway. It is surprising how far that approach has taken me over the years.

I seem to have made people laugh too, from a society doctor in New York, to members of the House of Lords. If you do things with no humour, you lose. If you can be funny and charming, you can get away with all kinds of things – sometimes without even meaning to. If you can make people laugh, you can probably make them like you, and sometimes you can even make them listen to you.

And I have worked hard: I have done what I have been asked to do and tried my best to do it well. The phrase I have always wanted to avoid above all others is, 'she's not up to the job.'

Above all, I have always tried to make the effort to make friends, and to find the fun in whatever situation I find myself in. That has got me into trouble at times, but it has also served me well.

I have had a lucky life, and I think I am still lucky now. I have had to give up some of the things that give me the most pleasure: smoking cigarettes; needlepoint and reading more recently when my eyes went; and dancing on tables now that I like to be in bed by ten. And I have been quite ill, which has taken away the great pleasure of eating. But even being ill has its upside, with all kinds of people, including lords from both sides of the House, showing me great warmth and kindness. And despite all of this, I am still having tremendous fun. I still get great pleasure from rattling around antique shops for bargains, and playing bridge with my old friends and going to the races. I rather enjoy my chocolate milkshake medicine. And secretly I am still hoping for one last stately little tap-dance in top hat and tails up on a table.

*

I want to use this opportunity to say thank you to some people who are very important to me. My years as Barker's wife were the happiest of my life and I am eternally grateful to him for giving me the love and affection I had craved since childhood.

The person to whom I owe the most in my professional life is the late Baroness Thatcher. It was Mrs Thatcher who put me in the Lords, and gave me my jobs. I will always be grateful for that.

I want to thank the many people in my life who continue to show me kindness: my hairdresser Bobby, my two lovely ladies who help me every week at Waitrose, my cleaner Lucy, the taxi drivers from Atlas who take me absolutely everywhere I need to go, my upstairs neighbours the Plaistows, and my great friends without whom I would be pushing up the daisies, the ever-helpful caretaker Garnet, assistant caretaker Val and plumber Len at my block of flats; at the House of Lords, I want to particularly thank the attendants to the chamber, the very helpful people who work at the post office in Central Lobby and in the finance office, the chefs and the wonderful Mary Rose in the dining room, and, of course, Black Rod. These people are near and dear to me: they make my life better every day through the kindness they show me. I want to acknowledge my huge debt of gratitude to every one of them.

Several people have been kind to me in helping me to write this book, principally Georgina Morley at Pan Macmillan and Deborah Crewe. It was Georgina who first suggested I should write a memoir. My first instinct was to ask, 'Could any sense ever be made of me?' followed by, 'And why on earth would anyone be interested in my doings?' However the redoubtable Ms Morley assured me all would be well on both fronts and then – wonderfully – produced Deborah Crewe who did her utmost to prove Georgina right – and as if that wasn't enough brought homemade soup with her on every visit to Battersea, which kept me going over a difficult summer. If you ever need a silk purse making out of a sow's ear I suggest you ask Georgina and Deborah.

Finally, I want to thank Adam. I imagine I am a most irritating mother, but he is the most wonderful son. He has always had guts and get-up-and-go and independence and courage, and I admire him enormously for it. He has shown great character in becoming what he has become.

I am very touched by the trouble he takes over me now, and full of love and gratitude towards him. My love and gratitude are also due to my daughter-in-law Elizabeth and my grandchildren Virginia and Christopher. I hope that this book will always remind them of me, and of the love that I have for them all.

*

I hope that this book is not boring. I couldn't bear that. I hope too that it isn't too rude. I do like to say what I think: I think it is terribly important to remain true to yourself. But the last thing I want is to upset anyone. I like a fight – especially a fight for something I believe in – but underneath it all, I am perhaps not quite as tough as I must sometimes seem.

CHAPTER ONE

A Glamorous Childhood

Childhood was not my happiest time. But when the war came and I was sent to Bletchley Park I grew up. Quite frankly, I've been happy ever since.

I never told anyone I was unhappy. One didn't. I had two younger brothers but I wouldn't have dreamed of confiding in them. Instead I became very self-contained about my feelings. My mother worked it out on the day she turned up at my boarding school unannounced and was greeted by the headmistress with more than the expected degree of surprise. Two weeks previously I had told everyone that my mother had died.

It wasn't my parents' fault. They were born in the nineteenth century and brought up by Victorians.

In fact my father, Arthur Campbell-Harris, hadn't really been brought up by his parents at all – he had barely known them. My grandfather was Surgeon General in India, and when my father was still a young boy he had been sent 'home' to live with relations and go to school in England (which he hated).

My mother, Doris Robson, was brought up as a sort of American princess: very very rich and rather spoilt. She never had to do anything for herself. Her father had come over to England from the United States in the 1880s and made an awful lot of money in the paint business and she was the heiress.

She and my father brought me up much as they had been brought up: it was simply how one did it then.

Young children led a nursery life, with mother and father sweeping in to say goodnight, all dressed up to go out for the evening with their friends in the Prince of Wales' set. Later, you were packed off to school. I didn't see much of them, and I found them rather frightening. There were no demonstrations of love and certainly no hugs.

My grandparents weren't demonstrative either – and not much use for confiding in. My father's mother came back from India after she was widowed and she terrified me. Once, as a teenager, I started to wear nail varnish to stop me biting my nails. My grandmother thought this was dreadful and called me 'a little nautch girl'. It's an Indian word. A nautch girl was a dancing girl, but she meant I looked like a tart probably. All I really remember about my mother's parents is my grandmother being deeply hurt and upset because my grandfather, whom she adored, was being horrible to her. Looking back I am sure he had Alzheimer's, which can make one terribly cruel to one's loved ones, but we didn't know about those things then.

I had nannies, of course. Nannies were often far more affectionate than one's relations. My first, lovely Nurse Toy, was a real old-fashioned nanny – she gave us lots of hugs – and I adored her. I can't truly remember much about her – I wish I could – except that I know, without a doubt, that I loved her and she loved me. But we were her last babies, and then she retired to Aldershot and that was that. The rest were just girls, really, who were horrid to me. They liked the boys and they couldn't be bothered with me.

My birth – on 23 October 1922 – was announced in *The Times*, of course. One of the other personal announcements that day was the thrilling news that Mr and Mrs Baron had changed their telephone number. Extraordinary, to think one put one's telephone number in the personal column of *The Times*. My parents knew the Barons, they made a fortune in cigarettes.

We lived in quite a large house when I was born. I only have one memory of it: having to be very very quiet because my brother David was being born.

My mother was in love with David, she really was. Me, she didn't much care for and the same was sadly true of Alastair, too, who came thirteen months after David. But David she adored and she treated him differently from everybody else. She called him Dimples. I longed for a nickname but she only ever called me Jean.

Soon after David was born we moved to a bigger house, 55 Great Cumberland Place, near Marble Arch. The whole of W1 was very much the smart part of London in those days, north of Hyde Park – Grosvenor Square and all those places. Everyone wanted to live there. Kensington and Chelsea were not posh at all then. Kensington was very much cheap flats for the respectable retired. A flat in Kensington was where you put grannies – particularly grannies who had been in India, because they had nowhere else to live, and no money. Genteel, but not smart. As for places like Battersea, I hadn't even heard of them and certainly didn't go there.

Great Cumberland Place was a Georgian townhouse: narrow and tall, with black railings and a white painted front. The kitchen was in the basement. On the ground floor was the hall, the dining room and my father's study. Up a half-landing was the drawing room and then up another half-landing was my mother's bedroom and my father's dressing room. The nursery area, where we children lived, was on the top floor. I remember leaning out of the top floor window with a penny wrapped in paper and throwing it down for the muffin man. At night,

I would watch the man who came to light the street lamps.

We ate all our meals in the day nursery although it was an awfully long way from the kitchen. There was a little lift to send the plates up and down but even so I think we were pretty unpopular with the kitchen.

We had a very good cook, mind you. And apart from her and nanny, there was a parlour maid, an under-parlour maid, about three cleaners, a governess, an under-nanny and a chauffeur. We didn't have a butler though. I don't know why and nor, to tell you the truth, do I know where they all slept – except the chauffeur: he had a cottage in the mews at the back. He was treated as a sort of head groom, really, which is probably what he had been before he became a chauffeur.

We were very handy for Hyde Park and Nanny often took us there for walks. My dearest companion at that time was my little black Scottie dog. He was such a dear little dog, and very good-tempered, putting up with the loving attentions of three little children. (And now that I think about it I have no idea how he managed, living with us on the top floor. What happened when he needed to go out to pee?) But one day the boys and Nanny were walking with him and he was stolen: he disappeared. They went off to Hyde Park together and came back without him. I was convinced that it wouldn't have happened if

I'd been there, and was absolutely heartbroken. Once we were walking in the park and I saw an airship flying overhead, the doomed R101. It was tremendously exciting. There were only two of them – the R100 and the R101 – so it was a very rare sight. They were terribly comfortable to be in, I think, but they were doomed. In 1930, when I was about eight, the R101 crashed over France and nearly everybody in it was killed.

Years later, during the war, number 55 was the only house in Great Cumberland Place to be bombed. We had left by that time, but of course I had to go back to have a look. The whole of the front of the house had been blown off and I could see my nursery wallpaper from the street. It must have been a really clean bomb though, because every other house had been left standing.

*

My parents moved in all the right circles, so it was, I suppose, a glamorous life. But of course as a child you don't know your life is different from anyone else's.

My grandmother was great friends with the Lloyd George family, and my mother was great friends with one of his daughters, Lady Carey-Evans, so we and the Lloyd George grandchildren on that side were all sort of brought up together. One of the granddaughters, Margie Carey-

Evans, was a bridesmaid at my parents' wedding. And later on, Robin Carey-Evans was a very close friend.

One of my mother's greatest friends was Lady Reading, who became my godmother. Her husband, Lord Reading, had been a member of Asquith's cabinet – the first practising Jew to be a member of the British government – and then Viceroy of India. My father had been his aide-de-camp, which was how he and my mother first met. Sadly, Alice Reading was an invalid all her life, but she still threw herself into charitable work, working with women and children and setting up hospitals in India. When they came back to London, the Readings lived in Curzon Street and we used to go there for tea. Lord Reading used to put balls of butter on the end of his very large nose, to make us laugh. We used to call the former viceroy our butter-nosed uncle.

After Alice Reading died, Lord Reading married Stella Charnaud, who had been his secretary in Delhi. Stella Reading was a tremendously energetic and active person. She founded the Women's Voluntary Service in the lead-up to the Second World War and in 1958 was appointed a life peer in her own right, becoming the first woman to take up her seat in the House of Lords. Baroness Swanborough, as she then became, took a great interest in all the staff working at the House of Lords and took enormous trouble to make sure they had proper facilities:

lavatories, places to wash their hands and so on. That is a great legacy for her because previously their lordships had really not taken any interest. I only knew her when I was a child – and in fact my main memory of her is that she had a heated loo seat at her house in Great North Street. But I think of her often.

There were other political friends, too. The Thorpes, for example. John Thorpe was a Conservative MP and his wife, Ursula – rather oddly, it seemed to me – always wore a monocle. Their son, Jeremy, who was a few years younger than me, would later become leader of the Liberal Party, although his career ended in scandal. As a child I spent quite a lot of time with Jeremy, although I actually thought he was rather a horrid little boy and we used to have terrible fights.

My parents were marvellous hosts and my mother, especially, always made sure everything was just so. I remember that one day there was a great fuss because the Maharani of Kapurthala was coming to lunch and my mother was serving rice and she wanted it to be properly cooked. The maharani had been a friend of my mother's since they were at finishing school together in Paris. Her name was now Maharani Prem Kaur but at that time she had been Anita Delgado, the beautiful and rather fast Spanish flamenco dancer, who had been spotted by the maharaja at the wedding of King Alfonso XIII of Spain.

The maharaja had decided he had to marry her, and had brought her to Paris to be wooed and educated.

*

While my mother enjoyed smart London lunches and cocktail parties, my brothers and I were in the nursery – or at school.

I was sent to endless posh schools. First, Miss Faunce's day school in Queen's Gardens, Bayswater, where there were two mistresses called Miss Cooke and Miss Kitchen, which was a big joke for us girls. Next, Miss Spalding's in Queen's Gate. By this time my brothers were going to school too, at Wagners, the boys' pre-prep school in Queen's Gate, and we used to fight all the way there on the top deck of the bus. I rather suspect my mother didn't pay the bills. I can't think why else I kept moving schools.

I also attended Miss Vacani's School of Dancing, where I learnt ballroom dancing and the correct way to curtsey when presented at court. Lessons took place in a big room on the first floor of a house in Knightsbridge, with all the nannies sitting upright and silent in chairs arranged around the edge of the room. Miss Vacani, who also gave private lessons to the young princesses Elizabeth and Margaret Rose, was not at all glamorous-looking. She was a tubby little person who wore the most impossibly high heels. Once a year she organized a charity matinee at the

Hippodrome Theatre and we all performed in front of our parents and nannies. There is a photo somewhere of me aged seven dressed as a Russian girl, and my brother David – who as a young gentleman was also expected to learn to dance – in a mauve suit. I danced the Tarantella that year and he had to dance as though in a nightclub. He didn't like the mauve suit at all.

Incredibly, after a year or two of Miss Vacani, my mother removed me and sent me to learn ballet with the Ballet Rambert, a serious ballet school whose prize ballerina was the famously beautiful Pearl Argyle. Goodness knows why my mother decided that this elephant she had given birth to was going to become a graceful ballet dancer but it did at least teach me rhythm.

Apart from school and dance lessons, Nanny took me skating at Grosvenor House once a week, which I loved; and my hair was done at Antoine's on Bond Street, which I didn't. My mother used to send me there on my own, early in the morning, because before nine o'clock it was half price. And I was made to have a perm, which I hated because in those days perms were ghastly, they just made your hair fuzzy. I was terribly shy and it made me feel sick inside being at the hairdressers just with grown-ups and all alone.

But then in 1929 came the Wall Street Crash. We lost everything. 55 Great Cumberland Place had to be sold – the prospectus devoted a whole page to a photo-graph of our big imported American fridge. We had had all this money and the most wonderful lifestyle and sud-denly we had nothing.

CHAPTER TWO

Rowling

We moved out of London to East Kent, to a house called Rowling. Rowling, like a lot of the land locally, was in the hands of the Lunacy Commission, because the lord of the manor was a lunatic and incapable of managing his own affairs. Because the Lunacy Commission couldn't sell the house, we could never buy it, only rent it, which would become a source of great sadness to me.

My father had come out of the army when he had married my mother, and gone into her father's paint business. I take my hat off to him because from having been ADC to the Viceroy of India, which was quite a grand kind of thing, he became the office boy in a paint factory and worked his way up to director. But until the Depression I don't think he had ever thought he would need to take his work at Indestructible Paint Ltd very seriously: he thought he had married money. I've got photographs of him from this time just sitting, with his hunting rifle and his dogs, looking utterly downcast.

My mother, who had never worked, decided to become an interior decorator. She had wonderful taste and she had friends who were still very rich, and she turned out to be rather an adventurous woman who liked change. She managed to build up a jolly good business.

My grandmother's life changed too, which must have been quite traumatic for my mother because she loved her mother dearly. She had been hugely rich, her husband having left her extremely well provided for, but it was all invested on the stock market. Now, suddenly, she had nothing: nothing at all. She came to live with us for a bit but that was never going to work for long, even though she loved my father and he was very nice to her (he was very nice with women generally – possibly too nice). In the end her brother-in-law, whose business was still thriving, gave her £1,000 a year, which she lived on pretty comfortably in a house off Eaton Square. But she never had her own money again.

Looking back, I realize that none of this actually made a big impression on me at the time. My eight-year-old's memory of the move isn't as a time of family crisis at all. But it must have been awful for the grown-ups.

*

Rowling was a charming house dating back to the sixteenth century in the village of Goodnestone. One entered into a hall with a huge walk-in fireplace and an incredible Charles II staircase. Off the hall were the dining room and the study and then the servants' quarters which were in their own wing at the back. It had great character and my mother gradually filled it up with beautiful things.

There was no heating or electricity at all for many years, only real coal fires for heat, and oil lamps for light. I thought it was lovely. We had lamps all over the house and elegant little boxes everywhere with salt in them. If one of the lamps flared up, you poured salt on it using a special spoon. We had a boy whose job it was to clean those lamps. He cleaned the lamps and he cleaned the shoes. And we had a gardener, of course, who also chauffeured sometimes – for some reason in an old London taxi. And my parents kept a small flat in Marylebone. So when I say we were poor, I suppose it was a bit like the Eton boy's story about poverty: 'There was this family. The father was poor. The mother was poor. The butler was poor . . .' We used to say my mother's idea of being poor was going to the Ritz on the bus. Life went on and in a curious way we went on living much as we always had and very grand people used to come and stay and they didn't seem to mind about the fires or the lamps.

Behind the house was a huge walled kitchen garden

and at the bottom of it a cottage where the gardener and his family lived. Beyond that was the farmyard, so if the wind blew in the wrong direction you got quite a hefty cow smell, which personally I didn't mind. The farmers who worked the land were a Scottish family called Hume who, like a lot of the East Kent farmers at that time, had come south to escape the abject poverty in Scotland. They were very good farmers but their accents were so strong we could hardly understand one another.

We only had one field. It had a nice hard tennis court in it, and I played a lot of tennis. Then there was the wood. The wood was one of the reasons my mother had been so entranced with the house. She had thought it was covered with lily of the valley but it wasn't, it was wild garlic. It looks quite similar – in fact it's very pretty – but you don't want to go travelling through it because the smell will knock you out.

*

For the first few years at Rowling, I went to a local school. Schools, in fact. School after school. When I was eleven I was sent away to boarding school, Princess Helena College. It was then in Ealing although it later moved to a lovely house called Temple Dinsley near Hitchin, where it still is today. It was named for Queen Victoria's third daughter and had been founded for the orphaned daughters of members of the armed forces and clergy. I hated it. I was dreadfully homesick, and I was unpopular. I felt that I was different from all the other girls, which is not a good thing as a child. You all want to be exactly the same.

I enjoyed all the creative things like art and acting, and I was very good at French, which was not me being clever but because I had had a French governess when we still had money. And I loved history and I read like mad. But I was hopeless at things like Latin and mathematics and so I didn't even try. I reckoned it was better to get five out of a hundred, which showed you hadn't tried, rather than twenty out of a hundred, which showed you had tried and failed. I didn't ever have cause to regret that approach: none of the things I didn't want to do, like maths, would ever have been useful to me later in life. I still believe that it is hopeless trying to make a child learn something he doesn't want to learn, and it is up to a child to reckon what will be useful to him in his life.

I wasn't hearty like the others, either. All the other girls had crushes on each other, and on the games mistress, which I didn't understand at all. I didn't want to crush on a woman and I didn't want to be crushed on. I used to go with the local boys into the woods and smoke instead. There was no sex, but a lot of smoking. I was really a most unsuitable person for English public school at that time.

The only person who was at all sympathetic to me was the headmistress. When I was sent as a punishment to stand outside her door, she used to ask me in and then we would sit on the floor and do jigsaw puzzles together – really big jigsaw puzzles like my mother used to do with her guests when the weather was bad and you didn't know what to do with them. (My mother was a member of a jigsaw puzzle club in Wigmore Street, a bit like a public library – you'd go there and pick up a puzzle for the weekend.)

I hated that school. Hate, hate, hate. It was not much fun to be unpopular at boarding school. But my family was not the kind of family where I could have gone to my mother and said, 'I am homesick.' I didn't confide in my parents; I practically called them 'sir' and 'ma'am'. So I bottled it all up until I was almost suicidally miserable, desperately waiting for the holidays to begin.

*

Holidays back at Rowling were spent walking in the woods, riding, and playing tennis.

I went for endless walks through East Kent with my brothers, picking mushrooms or just wandering about. We usually set off together but came back not together because we had had a flaming row on the way. I was the eldest and supposed to look after the boys. What this meant was that I was always in trouble. I got blamed for everything that went wrong, partly because I was the eldest and partly because my brothers were only thirteen months apart. As a result they were very close and they ganged up on me. I thought it might get better when they went to different schools – David to Eton and Alastair to Dartmouth Naval College, because by the time it was his turn my parents couldn't afford Eton – but that just meant they had more catching up to do in the holidays. Most days our wanderings would take in the village shop where we would buy cigarettes 'for our uncle' and then smoke them behind the pigsties.

It was a typical country life. We kept horses, which of course I loved, and ponies, and we rode to hounds with the West Street Hunt. My father, having been in the cavalry, wanted us all to ride but I am afraid I was the only one who was keen. We always had dogs, too. My greatest favourites were Ruby, a chocolate brown cocker spaniel, and Scarlett, a yellow Labrador. Ruby had several litters of puppies. When they were seven days old we cut off their tails. It isn't allowed now but in those days it was the done thing. It wasn't for fashion, contrary to what people stupidly say, but for a jolly good reason. Cocker spaniels are gun dogs and go bustling around in the undergrowth to retrieve the pheasants or partridge or whatnot. They were in and out of the thick bramble bushes all the time. Cocker spaniels have long tails which they wag enthusiastically to signal that they have found what they are looking for. Undocked, their tails get cut to pieces and cause the dogs great pain. So, even though it wasn't the nicest task, as there was always a lot more blood than I thought there would be, I held the puppies' tails while we cut them off.

We had regular shoots throughout the autumn, and what we shot we ate. Anything we couldn't eat was given away – to friends, to the farmers or to the gardener and his family. When the corn was cut, there always seemed to be even more rabbits and partridges than usual. The farmers would leave cutting the bit in the very middle of the cornfield until last, and then when they finally cut it all the rabbits and birds that had been hiding there came flocking out and we'd shoot them.

Ma taught herself to drive – in a fashion. It was quite an unusual thing for a woman at that time. We would all get into this enormous convertible and she would drive us down to Sandwich Bay. She didn't know how to turn round so the caddies at the golf course used to do it for her and then she would somehow or other drive us back. I don't know how we weren't all killed.

One consequence of our relative poverty, of which I

was terribly aware, was that after the crash my mother could no longer afford to buy me such beautiful clothes. Her friends the Barons (who had so helpfully announced their change of phone number in *The Times* on the day of my birth) had a daughter about the same age as me and I used to be given Betty Baron's cast-offs to wear. They came from Chanel, Lelong, all the top Paris couturiers, and they were wonderful garments. Sadly though, the Barons were very small. Betty was five foot tall and I was approaching six feet and not remotely the same shape as her. Wearing those things was agony: I could never even lift my arms.

I had two great friends at Rowling. One was a boy I called Ronnie, who was a year older than me and whose uncle lived at Knowlton, the big Elizabethan house opposite us. Ronnie lived in the village and his father used to take me hacking. Once he took me and Ronnie hacking, then for lunch and to the cinema. It was a heavenly afternoon. My parents gave Ronnie's father the most terrible blast, so he didn't ask me again. And Ronnie was just a friend, not a boyfriend – one didn't have such boyfriends in one's early teens in those days.

My other childhood friend was Anne Heywood, another only child. She was an awfully pretty girl and a wonderful golfer, known as the Golfing Babe of Kent. From her house in Sandwich Bay she could walk straight onto the Royal St George's golf course, and we used to play a lot of golf together, and ride ponies along the sand. I used to stay there a lot because it was easier for everyone than fetching me backwards and forwards. Anne contracted TB in 1939, before penicillin was available, and she was bedridden for months.

*

To my great regret, Rowling was never really ours. The Lunacy Commission finally decided that they did indeed want to sell it after all, but by that time it was almost the end of the war and my mother had moved on. We'd had to move out at the beginning of the war as Rowling had been requisitioned. The soldiers billeted there had torn down the Charles II staircase and done other terrible things. My mother was never one for standing still, let alone looking back.

During the war my mother had bought a ten-bedroom Queen Anne house called Spring Grove outside Wye, near Ashford in Kent. The local train-line went through Wye, Killem and Cartham to Canterbury so the local joke was, 'Why kill-em and cart-em to Canterbury?' Spring Grove was wonderful and I lost my heart again: absolutely covered in wisteria, with twenty acres of its own grounds, stone lions at the gates, and in a lovely position, opposite Wye Racecourse and with beautiful country all around. But we didn't stay there long either.

My mother loved buying houses, doing them up and then selling them. She had wonderful taste, and was very good at it, and she used them as showcases for her interior design business. But I can't say either her husband or her children liked it at all. Each time I loved whichever bedroom became 'my room' and each time it was heartbreak for me when we had to leave. If I hadn't been so frightened of my parents I would have turned around, the fourth or fifth time I was shown my new bedroom, and asked, 'For how long?' But I never did. My brothers and I never felt we had a real home to come back to – life would have been much, much easier if we had – and I developed an absolute, lifelong yearning to have my own home.

CHAPTER THREE

Finishing School

After the 'dead mother affair', I didn't go back to Princess Helena College. My mother had always intended that I should learn languages, as she had done as a girl. She spoke perfect French, German and Italian and was keen that I should do the same. Now, perhaps because she at last realized how unhappy I was at school, or perhaps because she realized there was a war coming, she brought her plan forward. At the age of fifteen, in 1937, I was sent to a French finishing school.

I had been to France before with my father. The first time was in the early 1930s, when I was about eleven, when my mother was in Switzerland. She was always too fat and, before she decided she simply couldn't be bothered, always on a diet. On this occasion, she went to a spa in the Alps, to do the 'cure', which was supposed to help her lose weight.

While she was in Switzerland, my father was to take

me to the South of France. I was terribly upset before we went because my mother, who chose all my clothes for the trip, had bought me a bathing suit that ended at my waist. It was like a boy's bathing trunks – there was no top. I was flat as a board but I didn't like to think so – I thought I was Mae West. We had bought everything at Fortnum & Mason and I was shocked when I went into the changing room to try everything on and it was full of naked ladies. I'd never seen anyone naked before.

My father and I stayed at the Hotel Eden Roc at Cap d'Antibes, which was glorious – and very posh. It was a sort of Mediterranean club for the rich and famous. It had a swimming pool carved out of the rock above the sea and I remember my father asking me to dive for him off the high diving board. I think I turned about three somersaults before I hit the water – I was very brave then – and he couldn't get over it. I loved it there. Every day we had lunch at Le Pam Pam, a stand-up cocktail bar in Juan-les-Pins where I had a hot dog and a glass of orange, and in the evenings a waiter would bring a tray of cold cuts to my room while my father went out on the town. Where, I now realize, he was very naughty indeed.

From the Eden Roc we went on to Biarritz where friends of my father had rented a villa. It was a different crowd there, although again very fashionable – the Prince of Wales and Mrs Simpson came to lunch in matching tweeds. I was allowed down to shake hands and then pushed back upstairs to the nursery. It didn't mean a thing to me at the time.

And in Biarritz, my father continued to be wildly unfaithful to my mother. Despite this, I think she really loved him. As a young woman she had had plenty of suitors: she was never considered a great beauty but she had a lively intellect, and there was a lot of money. During the First World War, she had a great friendship with the Canadian soldier and diplomat Georges Vanier, who had lost a leg fighting on the Western Front and was sent to convalesce at my grandmother's house in Cavendish Square, which had been requisitioned and turned into a nursing home. He became a diplomat after the war and in the 1950s became the Governor General of Canada. My mother might rather have enjoyed being the wife of the Governor General. But in any case, she had certainly had plenty of choice. Then she met my father and found – like every woman who met my father – that she adored him. He was frightfully good-looking.

They met in India in the early 1920s, at the residence of the viceroy. My father was of course serving as ADC to the viceroy, the Earl of Reading: after Malvern, he had gone to Sandhurst, and from there joined the 9th Bengal Lancers. My mother, having travelled round the world with only her Italian maid, which was very daring for the early 1920s, had been sent out to stay with the Readings, who were family friends. They met, they fell in love, they came back, they got married. They honeymooned in St Moritz, which my father said was dreadful because he had never skied before. My mother's mother had arranged it. It was probably the grandest thing she could think of.

As a child you don't really know quite what it is you are witnessing, or if you do you don't know what to do about it, but in his old age my father confessed it all to me.

One of his affairs was with an extremely beautiful woman who had been a Ziegfeld Follies girl. She married a very rich, very horrible man who was a rotten landlord (once, his tenants had all lined up holding rats and been photographed by the press) and then had a long affair with my father. In 1939 he took her to the Isle of Wight. I went on that trip too, and took photos that I annotated in my album: 'A memorable weekend spent at Seaview on the Isle of Wight'. I'm sure my mother knew what was going on but still, the conventions were kept.

There was also a story about my father at the wedding of Princess Marina and the Duke of Kent in 1934. My father was stationed on his horse as part of the mounted security on duty outside the Ritz and some woman in the crowd – I suppose she knew him – shouted at him, 'Come on over here Arty!' The whole crowd took up the call:

'Come on over here Arty!' and he had to be moved, because it was causing an uproar. He was livid and so was my mother. But again, nothing changed between them, publicly at least.

*

So now, in 1937, without having ever taken an exam, my formal education ended and I was sent to live with two old ladies, Mademoiselle Arbel and Mademoiselle Dettelbach. They had run a finishing school in Paris when my mother was a girl and she had been 'finished' there, and she persuaded them to come out of retirement for me: I think they were quite glad to have the money.

It was all very grand. The old ladies – I thought they were old but they were certainly a lot younger than I am now – lived in a huge white villa in Montrichard, a pretty village near Blois, with a cook, a maid and a gardener/chauffeur, and they treated me, their only charge, as *la jeune fille de la maison*. They taught me how to behave as a young lady in proper society – good manners, in other words, and how to make polite conversation – and a hell of a lot of French. I'd always spoken French because of the French governess, and now I managed to become bi-lingual. They took me around the sights of Paris and all the Loire chateaux. I took art lessons at a studio in Tours twice a week – chalks, pastels, oils, life drawing, whatever

I wanted, though I didn't have a great deal of talent — and played an awful lot of tennis. I'd always adored it and by this time I was a very good, left-handed tennis player. I had coaching all year round and there was serious talk of junior Wimbledon.

I didn't have much of a social life, but while I was at Montrichard I did meet Jean Borotra, the French tennis champion. He asked me out to dinner, but my mother found out and was horrified and forbade me from going. I was very upset because I was mad about tennis and he was the great name, but there you are, I wasn't allowed. To be fair to my mother I was only just sixteen and he must have been forty.

Mademoiselle Arbel was known as Pommé and it was her house, which she had had built when she retired. She was always immaculately and expensively dressed in hats and gloves and furs, and very splendid and slightly terrifying. Mademoiselle Dettelbach was known as Shoey and she gave the lessons. I felt sorry for her because Pommé really bossed her around and she had a miserable time.

After a year at Montrichard I was supposed to go on to Germany and then Italy, but my parents were increasingly concerned by the thought of a coming war, so instead I went to Paris for a year and learnt my German there.

I stayed with a Mme de Benouville in her huge house

on one of the roads leading off from the Étoile. My pre-
occupations were much as they had been at Montrichard:
tennis lessons, art lessons and now German lessons, to
all of which I had to be chaperoned as I was considered
too young to go about Paris on my own. There were
other girls staying with Madame, too, so my social life
took off a little bit then, although the others were older
than me so no one thought me much worth thinking
about. But the suave Pierre de Benouville, the son of the
lady who put us all up, was a particular hero of mine. I
thought he was the cat's whiskers. And in fact all the
girls thought he was heaven, but he was a member of
Action Française which was very very right-wing and not
very well thought of.

I'd been in Paris for six months or so when my parents
and brothers came to France for a family holiday, for the
Easter of 1939. David was down from Eton, Alastair from
Dartmouth. By 30 May, Joan of Arc's Feast Day, they
were all still in Paris. Even though I was much too young
my mother had somehow managed to insist that I should
take part in the Cortège Traditionnel, an annual procession that lays flowers at the statue of Joan in the Place
des Pyramides. I thought it was a frightful nuisance but
she was quite right because one never had the chance
again. The war and the fall of Paris weren't far off by this
time and the photos of the procession, with tanks and

cavalry in the background, are quite poignant. But there was no poignancy at the time. I was already terribly tall – especially compared to the French girls – and I remember that as I processed a lady said to me, 'Mademoiselle, get off your ladder,' before lifting my skirts and poking my legs. I was furious.

Throughout that summer of 1939 my mother became increasingly convinced that there would be a war and in August she insisted that I leave Paris, with a promise that if she was wrong and all turned out well, I could go back. I did return, but not until 1946.

CHAPTER FOUR

Lloyd George's Land Girl

I was in Canterbury Cathedral on 3 September 1939, the day the war started. That was nothing unusual: we often went there for Sunday services. It was a sunny day and shafts of late summer light shone through the stained-glass windows as we gathered for matins. The Very Reverend Hewlett Johnson, known as the Red Dean for his strong pro-Soviet views, was in the pulpit when the sirens went off, very loud and very menacing. The dean shepherded us all down to the crypt, where matins proceeded as usual and as though our lives had not just fundamentally changed. Just as he finished, the all-clear sounded. It had been dreadfully frightening because we were near the coast, and we really didn't know what we were going to find as we emerged from our subterranean vault. But of course nothing had happened and we all went home. And so our war began.

Rowling was quickly requisitioned by the military

and my parents had to decamp to their flat on Mansfield Street in Marylebone. David, who was then fifteen, was sent from Eton to the United States, where he attended Exeter School in New Hampshire and lived with relations in Chicago during the holidays. Alastair, aged fourteen, was left at the naval school at Dartmouth. But my parents didn't quite know what to do with me. I was sixteen, nearly seventeen. I couldn't very well go back to Paris: my finishing had to be abandoned, unfinished. I was too young to join up, and there was no room for me in the Marylebone flat.

Someone, however, thought it would be a good idea for me to become a land girl on Lloyd George's farm at Churt in Surrey. My mother must have appealed to her great friend, Olwen Carey-Evans, LG's daughter. It solved the problem of what to do with Jean at the same time as letting Lloyd George show that he was doing his bit for the war effort.

In a way, the outbreak of war was the end of our family life. Rowling was gone and we children were touted out around the place – thrown out into the world, I remember thinking – and my parents sort of gave up doing things for us.

My mother didn't see David again – the eldest son she so absolutely adored – until he was eighteen years old and six foot five. They thought Alastair was quite OK,

too, and didn't need bothering with, but he did need
bothering with, and love. And I was just a bloody nuisance.
It didn't strike me at the time but looking back it was
pretty awful the way we were left to fend for ourselves.
Perhaps it's one of the reasons that, although I seem quite
tough, I am actually quite easily upset.

*

Lloyd George was in his late seventies when the war broke
out. He had always had a reputation as a great ladies'
man: during the Great War, Lord Kitchener is supposed
to have said that he tried to avoid sharing military secrets
with the cabinet, as they would all tell their wives, apart
from Lloyd George, who would tell someone else's wife.
By this time it was an open secret – at least open to me
as a friend of the family – that the old boy lived at Churt
with his long-term mistress, Frances Stevenson, who was
also his personal secretary and had previously been a
governess to LG's daughter Megan. (In 1943, after his
first wife, Margaret, died, Lloyd George – aged eighty –
married Miss Stevenson.)

The living arrangements at Churt reflected the unusual
circumstances. In the early 1920s Lloyd George had had
a grand country house built – an Edwardian-style villa
with a big picture window looking out over the orchards
– which he had named Bron-y-de. He now spent most of

his time there. The house was surrounded by Green Farm: hundreds of acres of farmland and apple orchards, dotted with cottages where the farm workers lived, together with his political staff who had been billeted there. Miss Stevenson lived not in the house and not in a cottage but instead in a very luxurious and tastefully furnished two-bedroom bungalow, with a portrait of her in the big open drawing room. However, when the family wasn't around – which was most of the time – she spent her time up at the house.

I was put to live with Miss Stevenson – or Flossie, as Lloyd George's family called her, though not to her face. To my surprise (because I had imagined some kind of femme fatale) Miss Stevenson wasn't at all glamorous: she looked exactly like someone's governess. Nor did she give the impression of being at all ambitious, though I suppose she must have been. In fact, when she was there and not up at the house with LG, Miss Stevenson was incredibly kind to me; she was a very good listener. Unfortunately, Miss Stevenson's two chows, Helen and Beauty, were very very mean. Chows *are* mean, usually – I don't know why on earth she liked them. I had been allowed to take my rather ageing but beloved cocker spaniel, Ruby, with me to Churt, to keep me happy. But the poor girl was an interloper and she was badly bullied by the chows who used to sit on her, so I had to send her back to my parents.

Not long after that my father took me out to lunch to tell me my darling Ruby had died.

Being at Churt was desperately dull. I had no social life at all. All the young farm workers had joined up and I was the one and only land girl so there was no one there my age. Apart from Miss Stevenson, who was then in her late fifties, there were a bunch of old men, and Jennifer, Miss Stevenson's daughter, who was a fuzzy-haired child of ten or eleven. (Jennifer's parentage remained mysterious long after Lloyd George died. While I was there she called Lloyd George 'Taid', which is Welsh for 'Grandfather'.) There were some secretaries, too. I bit one of them once. How awful to admit it, even now. I was doing the washing up and she said something so rude to me that I seized her arm and bit it. Of course, now all I can remember is the bite, not what she actually said. I've never bitten anyone else, I'm happy to say.

There weren't even any animals there on the farm, which I would have loved. It was all fruit. I picked apples and packed apples and unpacked apples and repacked apples. Each and every apple was wrapped in paper and then the apples were packed into bushel baskets. It was endless. Occasionally, to relieve the tedium, I picked 'Lloyd George' raspberries (the variety was named after LG). There's a photo of me and Lloyd George with his farm manager, inspecting some raspberries and looking very agricultural. It was of course all got up for the gentlemen of the press, but I have a signed copy in my sitting room all the same.

The only animals to be found – apart from Miss Stevenson's beastly chows – were the bees in the apiary and I got so desperate for something to do that I did once dress up in all the gear and go to see the bees. We didn't get on terribly well though. Certainly I wasn't going to find them as amusing as horses or dogs, or even pigs or cows, would have been. Some of their honey was used to make mead – which I think is disgusting stuff but I suppose if you are crazy about honey you might like it. The honey and the mead were then sold on to Harrods and Fortnum & Mason, with labels saying 'From the Estate of David Lloyd George OM MP'.

There was absolutely nowhere to go and nothing to do. Occasionally, Lloyd George would ask me up to the house – where the old goat would stand me up against a wall, take out a tape measure and try to take all my measurements; it was never explained why and because he was my boss and the grandfather of my buddies I didn't dare ask – or he would go up to London and I would get a lift in his chauffeur-driven Rolls Royce. But these were rare outings.

It was all a rather dramatic change of pace for me after tennis coaching and art studios and touring the chateaux of the Loire and meeting lots of longed-for Frenchmen.

After about a year of nearly dying of boredom I persuaded my parents to let me come back to London and take a secretarial course. The course was in London but my parents didn't want me living there because of the bombs, so I was sent to live with my mother's awful old Uncle Edward, who was then in his late seventies. Uncle Edward had been the head of Pinchin Johnson, a very successful paint and varnish company then in the FT 30, which was the forerunner to the FTSE 100. He owned a wonderful house on Avenue Road just north of Regent's Park. One entered the grounds through iron gates and proceeded past a lodge and up a long drive. There were two-and-a-half acres of gardens – where I had buried my canary when it died – with outhouses, and stables, and garages, and a Regency bandstand and greenhouses with the best grapes I have ever eaten, anywhere. Beautiful, beautiful grapes. Imagine, all of that in the middle of St John's Wood. But I wasn't sent to live with old Uncle Edward in St John's Wood, alas. I was sent to live in his house in Sunningdale, in Berkshire, where he was waiting out his war playing golf.

My mother's mother had decamped to Sunningdale from her house in Eaton Square by this time too so it was quite the exciting party – me and two septuagenarians.

That said, there were some exciting plans at one point. Before the war, Uncle Edward had thrown a huge party every year and all of London used to come down for it. There was dancing outside, and gambling inside – roulette and so on. I had never had any part in the parties because I was still too young. It was now rather thrillingly suggested that I should have an eighteenth birthday party at the same time as ghastly Uncle Edward's eightieth. Somehow, though – perhaps because of the war – it didn't happen.

It was certainly thanks to the war that I was sent to Sunningdale. My parents thought I'd be safe there, but I wasn't safe at all. The day I arrived, a German bomber being chased by a British squadron emptied all its bombs over Sunningdale as it tried to escape. Sunningdale is built on a very steep hill with the golf course at the top, and one of the bombs blew a lorry driver from the main road about a mile up the hill, past the railway station and right to the top. I don't know whether the bomber escaped eventually or not, but I do know the body of the lorry driver was found on the practice tee of the ladies' course. It frightened me so much that I slept in a cupboard under the stairs for three weeks.

However, there was nothing to be done. So in Sunningdale I stayed, and up to London I went every day to do my secretarial course at the Triangle, a secretarial

college in South Molton Street. I learnt to type and, tech-
nically speaking, I learnt how to do shorthand, but I was
always hopeless at it. Hopeless. I travelled there and back
by bus, until one day, while I was waiting at the bus stop,
a car stopped and out got two chaps in uniform, saying,
'Anybody going to London who'd like a lift?' In I got
with these two strange men. The next day they were there
again and in I got again, and it became a regular thing,
every day. They would pick me up at Hyde Park Corner
and drive me back to Sunningdale, too. When my mother
found out I think she was very shocked and not at all
happy about it, but she couldn't stop me. So instead she
checked up on them and discovered that they were very
respectable, which made her much happier. But she really
needn't have worried. Nobody made a pass, nobody did
anything; they were just terribly kind and it was rather
lovely for me not to have to take the bus.

But that was the extent of the excitement. From
September 1939 until October 1940 I was having my
own phoney war and it was very dull indeed.

CHAPTER FIVE

Bletchley Park

In October 1940 I turned eighteen. I was going to need something to do once my secretarial course finished but I was still below conscription age, and having worn one at school for all those years I certainly didn't want to go back into uniform. As usual, my parents went around saying, 'I'm not sure what to do with Jean.' One day, my father said it to a friend who was a lieutenant commander in the navy.

'Well,' said the friend. 'I know someone who works at Bletchley. Why don't you think about that?'

A few days later – and at the time I didn't know that it had anything to do with my father or the lieutenant commander – I found myself sitting across a table from a frightfully grand man called Frank Birch, at the Lyons Corner House at the corner of Whitehall and Trafalgar Square. We ordered coffee and he asked me if I spoke German. I said yes. He asked me, did I speak French, and

I said yes to that too. What about Italian? I said not really but I could have a try. He gave me something to translate, which I did. 'Well,' he said, 'you'll do. Here's your ticket, take the train tomorrow morning to Bletchley.' And that's what I did – without knowing anything about anything. I spent the next five years working at Bletchley as part of the team devoted to German Naval Codes. In those years I made great friends, I had a great deal of fun, and I grew up.

When my suitcase and I arrived at Bletchley Park the following day it looked nothing like it would come to look later in the war, and nothing like it does now. At that time Bletchley Park consisted of the red brick mansion house and a few Nissen huts. I never went into the mansion by the way and never knew what went on there. It was known to us simply as 'the other side'; I think it was military intelligence. That was the way it was: you did your work with blinkers on.

I signed on – which meant signing the Official Secrets Act – and was taken to one of the Nissen huts, Hut 4, where a tall, old man called Edward Green (and known, it seemed, as 'Daddy Green') appeared to be in charge of a group of about six girls. I sat at a typewriter immediately and started typing away. And so there I was.

At the end of my shift I was shown to my transport – a Ford shooting brake driven by a uniformed girl from the Military Transport Corps and stuffed with six other girls – and taken with my fairly large suitcase to my billet, in a railway worker's cottage. (Incidentally, Bletchley was on what was then known as the 'Varsity Line' – the trains ran direct to both Oxford and Cambridge, which was very useful from the point of view of all the dons who were working there.)

I didn't meet the railway worker, but I met his wife, who seemed very nice. She showed me around and I noticed that there was no lock on the bathroom door. 'Oh,' I said, 'what about the bathroom door?' 'Well that's all right, don't worry,' she said. 'When you're having a bath my husband will be on the lines so he won't be around.' I plunged into a bath on the first night and in comes the husband. On purpose, without a doubt. I changed my billet pretty rapidly after that.

After the embarrassment of the railway worker's cottage I rather fell on my feet with my billets. My second was at Great Brickhill, with the ancient widow of a rather well-known Edwardian author called W. J. Locke, who kept Pekinese dogs. We got along very well together – she had her Pekineses and me – and I was extremely comfortable. The house was small but cosy, with a well-kept garden, in a pretty village up a hill behind Bletchley, and I had a decent-sized room with twin beds. Sadly, however, I did something a bit silly. I took pity on a friend who wasn't happy in her digs and persuaded Mrs Locke to take her in as well. It was a disaster. Mrs Locke hated her. My poor friend had to move out, and as I had brought her in I felt I had to go with her.

But boy did I luck out the third time, because I was billeted with the family of an extremely rich banker. He was called George Ansley, and his home was Passenham Manor, a very splendid early seventeenth-century stone manor house. Suddenly I had horses to ride, chickens to feed and very little sign of food rationing anywhere. Although they used to argue bitterly with each other, the Ansleys were very kind to me: I think they saw me as their war work. They wouldn't accept any rent, which meant thirty bob a week more for me, and Mr Ansley taught me all about wine, and they introduced me to all their friends, who would come down for the weekend, and who became my friends. One friend had two boyfriends and she would bring one of them one weekend, and then the next weekend she would bring the other. She married one of them in the end and became an ambassador's wife, which also came in very handy later on. I was terribly spoilt.

*

Life at Bletchley was a mix of the deathly dull and the thrillingly exciting. When we weren't working hard we were being extremely naughty.

The daily routine was very circumscribed: one went to the hut one worked in, left the hut only to visit the canteen, did one's work, and then took the transport back to one's billet. One did not wander around the place or talk to anyone outside one's section. Day after day, week after week, month after month, that was the routine. People spent their whole war in one room.

The job itself was deeply tedious: we were cipher clerks and we simply typed. We had to transcribe German naval code from a tape in five-letter groups, each one with a Z at the front, and it was extremely repetitive. Once we had finished transcribing the code, it was sent across the corridor to the team in the room opposite. I still don't really know what happened to the code once it got there. You didn't ask, you just did. The team our codes went to was headed up by Walter Ettinghausen, one of two Jewish brothers working at Bletchley. Walter was fat, jolly and rather good-looking but you didn't mess around with him. (Well, I'm afraid we did mess around of course, and he was always furious about it.) Ernest, his younger brother, headed up one of the shifts and was not nearly as attractive. At the end of the war Ernest went on to work in GCHQ. Walter emigrated to Israel, changed his surname to Eytan and set up a school to train members of the new country's foreign service, eventually becoming director general of the

Foreign Ministry. I suspect that nothing that happened at Bletchley was ever a secret from the Israelis.

The food was awful. I got a tapeworm from the Bletchley Park pork and was in the Middlesex Hospital in an isolation ward being starved for a week to get rid of the thing. It was about fifteen feet long when it finally came out.

But the worst thing was working shifts. It was awful. You worked nine to six, four to midnight, or midnight to nine, and they changed the shift every week, so you could never get into a proper sleep pattern. I have never to this day understood why they didn't do what nurses do and keep us on the same shift pattern for three months. I was tired all the time.

But despite being exhausted and often really quite bored, I did make some very close friends.

The transport to and from Bletchley Park every day was the opportunity – the only opportunity really – to meet people outside one's section. I met my great friends Osla Benning and Sarah Norton on the way to work. They were billeted together at the White Horse Inn and they went about as a pair, having previously worked together making aeroplanes at a Hawker Siddeley factory. Both of them were grand and very beautiful.

Sarah, or Sally, was three years older than me and the daughter of the 6th Lord Grantley. She had learnt her fluent German in Munich before the war, where she and her girlfriends used to sit in the Carlton Tea Rooms and pull faces at Adolf Hitler and his cronies across the room. She and Osla both worked for the Ettinghausen brothers. Sally had 'come out' and done the season in 1938 but despite her eighteen-inch waist and perfect legs hadn't found a husband by the time the war started.

It was Sally who introduced me to Max Beaverbrook, the enormously powerful Anglo-Canadian newspaper tycoon and politician who had been Minister of Information during the First World War and held various positions including Minister of Supply during the Second. Sally's mother had been Max's mistress and had a cottage up at Cherkley, his country house just outside Leatherhead. When she died, just before the end of the war, I went with Sally to help pack up her belongings. We had dinner with the old boy. It was the first time I'd met him but funnily enough I managed not to be intimidated at all. In fact I seemed to be a great success. I went there quite a lot after that: he would send me my rail ticket from Bletchley or London and I would go and spend the weekend there, and meet absolutely everybody because he gathered them all around him. It was riveting. And of course he lived like an absolute prince, with a private cinema and whatnot. He gave fabulous dinner parties too. It was really living it up; it's almost unimaginable looking back to think that it was wartime. I'm sure one of the reasons he invited me was the family connection with Lloyd George. Beaverbrook was always asking me about LG – and about Miss Stevenson, who was then a figure of mystery to all the politicians and newspaper people. I didn't really know what I could tell him: I just kept saying she was very nice.

On one visit to Cherkley during the 1945 general election campaign I did some of my best sucking up ever. There was a popular song about the Canadian government's alcohol restrictions doing the rounds:

> *Sing a song of sixpence*
> *A bottle full of rye*
> *Six and twenty ounces*
> *For a month's supply*
> *When the war is over*
> *We'll all begin to sing:*
> *'Now we've finished Hitler*
> *Where's Mackenzie King?'*

Mackenzie King was the prime minister of Canada, and Max Beaverbrook was originally Canadian, of course. After dinner, I sang a different version:

> *Now the war is over*
> *We can all relax.*
> *No more Mr Hitler*
> *Lots and lots of Max.*

He loved it.

Years later, when I was living in the United States, the phone rang and it was Max. 'Jean,' he said, 'come and spend Christmas with me.' 'I can't,' I replied, 'I'm going to my family.' Max said, 'Bring them.' And when I said, 'I don't think they'd like that,' he put the telephone down and never spoke to me again.

Sally and I were great pals, but I think Osla was my dearest friend. She was a delight. Spoilt rotten, but adorable and loved by everyone. She had dark hair and fair skin and was simply beautiful. Her mother had no home but lived in a permanent flat in Claridge's and had had five husbands.

Apart from Sally and Osla, my closest friend at Bletchley was Jean Graham. Jean worked in a related hut and although we didn't work directly together I sort of knew what she was doing, the way one often does even though one is not meant to. Jean and I were both tall — we were actually the same size, so we used to swap clothes. We doubled our wardrobes at a stroke, which was marvellous; they were pretty limited because of clothes rationing. She was born blue-blooded and everybody in her family was a duke (she was related to the whole damn lot of them, mainly through her mother) but she never had any money. Years later, she ended up having to sell her estate on the Isle of Arran. In fact there's quite an amusing story about that. The first time Jean thought she'd sold it she rang me up. 'Guess where I am? I'm in Claridge's. Come on round, we'll have a glass of champagne and celebrate selling Arran.' So round I went and we drank a lot of champagne and had a very merry time. The next day she rang me up again and said, 'You won't believe it. He's reneged on the deal.' So not only had she not sold Arran but she had a night at Claridge's and the champagne and God knows what else to pay for. Awful.

While we were at Bletchley, we girls did everything we could think of to lighten our lives and I am afraid I often behaved very badly indeed.

We all had party pieces that we would perform for each other if the night shift was slow. Mine was 'Chattanooga Choo Choo': 'Pardon me, boy, is that the Chattanooga Choo Choo?' Lovely. Actually that was still my party piece fifty years later when I was a minister. I still know every word. We would also send out false notices. One went 'In future all female personnel will wear hats to work.' It was all quite idiotic, and a bit childish. But we were children really.

Once, Osla and Sally bundled me into a large laundry basket on wheels that was used to move secret files and then pushed it down the corridor. It's not true, though it has been said, that I went careering into the gents' loo. In fact, I went straight into the office that was right at the end of the corridor. The occupant of the office, Geoffrey Tandy, had already decided he did not like me and now he was absolutely furious. As a punishment, the three of us were taken off the same shift and it took us three weeks to get back together again at work.

Another time we all stood and sang the 'Horst Wessel Lied'. *'Die Fahne hoch! Die Reihen fest geschlossen!'* It was the Nazi Party anthem and the German national anthem and I knew the whole thing. (Still do now. In fact, I sang it to a German doctor who I was sent to see just a few months ago and he was utterly shocked and furious.) Walter Ettinghausen was appalled. Well, he was right to be. I agreed with him, even then; I thought we were dreadful. But we were very young and terribly bored.

Whenever we could we rushed up to London and danced all night, then ate enormous breakfasts at a Lyons Corner House, with almost everything ersatz – fake scrambled eggs, fake everything. And then the chaps would see us to Euston Station and we would take the milk train and go straight back to work. I had one dress, from Fenwick, and a black fur coat which I had bought with money I'd been given for my sixteenth birthday. It cost £15 and it looked lovely but it was skunk and if it got wet, it smelt. But I wore it through thick and thin, so I guess I just smelt. I had several things made out of curtains, too, because curtain material wasn't rationed.

My friend Robin Carey-Evans, Lloyd George's grandson, came in very useful as a companion on those occasions. He was a bomber pilot and we always went out together when we could both get leave. I suppose you could say that he was my first boyfriend, but it was always more of a friendship than a love affair. I was very fond of him but I didn't want to go to bed with him: it would have spoilt the friendship. He seemed happy with that too: we danced all night with no complications whenever I was up from Bletchley and he had come down from his bomber. He lives in Australia now and we still write.

We always went to the 400, a nightclub on Leicester Square that doesn't exist any more. We had such happy parties there. It was very small and you had to be a member. Inside there was a stage for the band – it was all live music, of course – a dance floor, and a number of small round tables. There was a wonderful head waiter there whom everybody loved. (His son became an MP and was made a 'Sir' and doesn't like to be reminded that his father was a waiter. But he was a jolly good one, so why not?) I was horrified once though, because I was at one table with a boyfriend and I looked round and saw my brother at another table with a girlfriend. That was bad enough. But then I looked round again and there, at a third table, was my father. With a girlfriend.

On 23 October 1943 I held my twenty-first birthday

party at the 400. I don't remember an awful lot about that evening but I still have a wonderful piece of paper signed by everyone who was there: Robin, Osla, Sally, Anne Heywood, and my brother David included. In fact I think I must have celebrated my twenty-first birthday there twice because I also kept a second piece of paper dated August 1943 and with a wonderfully witty drawing on it. It was also signed by those present: Osla, Sally and all.

We also used to go to The Embassy, on Old Bond Street. Or the Bagatelle, a French restaurant with a dance floor where they used to play a special tune the moment they saw me coming in. Just imagine: what heaven. And there was another rather naughty one where the girls were tarts really. Don't ask me where that one was. I don't know. I never went there.

We really were awfully pure. None of us went to bed with anybody. You didn't do it. The boys tried, of course, but no, we weren't brought up that way. The most we did, was that from time to time we used to go out of the 400 and sit on a bench in Leicester Square and neck. But we'd be hanging onto our knickers as hard as we could.

I didn't formally 'come out'. Presentations at court stopped during the war. But I did go to the Queen Charlotte's Ball. The Queen Charlotte, traditionally, had been where well-bred girls had been launched into society each year with an introduction to the monarch of the day. Then they attended all the season's parties and balls and – with any luck – met a suitable husband. In 1941 it was held at Grosvenor House on Park Lane.

Afterwards, my companion and I headed across Mayfair to the Café de Paris, on Coventry Street near Piccadilly. It was a high-class place and a lot of famous people and members of the royal family went there. During the Blitz people went there even more because the dance floor was in the basement and they felt safe from the bombs. What they didn't realize was that it had a glass roof. That particular night, as we got near to the Café we were held behind a police cordon. The Café had received a direct hit: the young bandleader Snake Hips Johnson, and most of his West Indian Orchestra and a lot of the people dancing had been killed. I knew a beautiful woman who survived but she lost a leg. Imagine. If we had been half an hour earlier, we would have been there, so we were very lucky.

Instead, my beau hired a taxi and told the driver, 'Twice round the park and drive slowly.' I ought to have known better. I said to my mother afterwards, 'I don't think people have tried to kiss me that way before.' She said, 'I don't much care for it either.'

If I missed the train to town I would hitch-hike. I was lucky that I never got into trouble. It wasn't that I was oblivious to the dangers: I knew them well. I was just prepared to take a chance, to get myself up to London.

There was one particular time when I could see a left hand wandering off the gear stick and getting ready to pounce, so I scrunched myself into the corner and tried awfully hard to sound casual. Nothing happened. I think my voice might have put him off, because I clearly wasn't common. He might have thought that if he did something to me there would be some comeback.

I must occasionally have gone to Kent instead of London when I had leave because I remember riding ponies on the beach with Anne Heywood (now thankfully recovered from TB). It was fascinating because all the flotsam and jetsam would be washed up from ships that had been sunk. One cargo was nothing but lavatory seats. Another was nothing but cheese. And the whole of the town used to come out and pick up whatever there was and cart it back to Sandwich. After the war Anne married and moved up north and I never saw her again. Isn't that sad?

*

Security was of course of supreme importance at Bletchley. We were sworn to secrecy. It was absolutely drummed into us and we took it very very seriously. Curiously, we kept quiet for so long that even now, when we are allowed to talk, I still find it hard, except when I'm with others who were there. But we are a sadly dwindling group; there are fewer and fewer of us. Some people found it terribly difficult not being able to tell their families what they were doing, but my parents weren't actually terribly interested so for me it wasn't difficult at all. When our boyfriends asked us what we did, we had a pact that we would tell them we were the girls who decided who got medals. So we were very popular with the boys.

It was because of the need for secrecy that everyone was kept to their individual sections. Occasionally though, one was asked by a senior member of the section to deliver a message. And that was how I came to meet Alan Turing, the inventor of the Bombe machines that were kept in special huts. Even then, when no one was supposed to know what anyone else at Bletchley Park was doing, I knew that he was an important man whose mathematical genius and inventions had enabled us to finally break the German naval codes. I cannot claim that I knew him – I wish I had – or that we'd had so much as a conversation, because I'm not sure he even said thank you. But I did once deliver a message to him.

However, despite the importance of the work and the need for great secrecy, there was no vetting. As far as I know, they didn't do any checks on me. Actually, now I think about it, it was because they were snobs. With us Foreign Office people, they assumed that if you spoke the Queen's English and had been to the right schools you were a reliable person, which is absolute rubbish, of course.

When I arrived at Bletchley in 1941 there were about 400 people working there. By the time I left there were more than 6,000. The scattering of Nissen huts had been replaced by large concrete blocks, so that Hut 4, where I worked, was no longer in a hut at all. A lot of the expansion was due to the arrival of the Americans, who rather took over after the United States joined the war. We weren't much good at monitoring the Japanese U-boats though. The only thing I can remember in Japanese is 'maroo', which I always thought was Japanese for ship but I am now told means 'circle'. The Americans seemed to have an entirely different concept of security from ours. The moment they arrived, *Life Magazine*, which was like *Hello!* is today, was suddenly full of a long article all about our work on the Japanese codes, which upset us terribly: we thought it was an appalling security risk.

When the transport picked us up each day, we had to give our names before we were allowed to get in the car. When the Americans first arrived, a chap waiting for the transport said, 'I'm Friendly.' 'Well,' said the girl driving our transport, 'you may be friendly, but you're not getting in my car. Tell me your name.' That was Al Friendly, who became a great friend, and who, fifteen years later, became editor of the *Washington Post*.

*

My father was fifty years old by the time war broke out and too old to serve in the regular army. Because my parents' London flat was on Mansfield Street, in Marylebone, he became the commanding officer of the Marylebone Home Guard, which took in the BBC, the whole of Harley Street, and a lot of other amusing people too.

All the top Harley Street doctors and surgeons joined my father's home guard as ordinary troops. They were absolutely terrible at parades and putting on battledress and so on because any form of togetherness was anathema to them: they were all used to being the king of their own little world. My father didn't think the BBC's defences were up to much either. He was convinced that a couple of enemy parachutists would be able to take out our national broadcaster without much trouble. To show them how lax they were, he decided to capture the BBC himself. He issued fake passes to some of his men and they attacked, quite easily making it into the Holy of Holies.

There were all kinds of celebrities in my father's home guard. Bud Flanagan, who with his partner Chesney Allen was a hugely popular comedian and singer, was put on patrol on a street corner once, but such a vast crowd gathered around just to look at him that my father was never able to put him on duty in public again.

Vivian Van Damm, the chap who managed the Windmill Theatre, was also in my father's unit. The Windmill Theatre was the first theatre in twentieth-century London to find a way of putting naked girls on stage. They got the then Lord Chamberlain, the 2nd Earl of Cromer, whose office acted as the official censor for theatres throughout the country, to agree that if nude statues weren't rude, then nude girls couldn't be rude, so long as they weren't moving. Lord Cromer pronounced: 'It's all right to be nude, but if it moves, it's rude.' And he used to come personally to inspect each new show to check that it was acceptable. So girls were presented in a series of poses in 'tableaux vivants'. The next innovation was the fan dance. A nude girl would dance around while two clothed girls held fans in strategic places. Then at the end of the dance the fans would be removed as she stood, stock-still and statuesque, for ten seconds.

The Windmill was proud of the fact that even at the height of the Blitz, the theatre remained open. Indeed, its motto became 'We Never Closed'. But at least once a year it did close – to the public at least – and the owner gave the members of the Marylebone Home Guard their own private show. I am sure that they all got terribly drunk and that it was all quite disgusting. My mother, rather sensibly, would go to the country that weekend.

I never went on the big home guard night, but I did once go to an ordinary show there, because I had never been to a naked theatre and I wanted to see what happened. I wasn't terribly interested in what was going on onstage – it wasn't for me – but I was quite interested in what went on in the audience. There would be five or six performances a day and although some people would stay all day, others left after one performance, or even in the middle of a performance if the act became boring (there was comedy as well as naked girls). At that point, the men at the back of the theatre would scramble to get the seats at the front, climbing over the seats rather than going out and around. This was known, I gathered, as the 'Windmill Steeplechase'.

My mother's war was much less glamorous. She worked in a factory in Kent but still spent a good deal of time up in London, either at the flat, or at a room in her bridge club at the bottom of Park Lane. One day, on her way to catch a train to work, very early in the morning, she fell and ruptured her Achilles tendon. She lay in the street outside Selfridges for hours. Eventually, she was taken to hospital, where of course they did what they could, but she was on crutches for the rest of her life.

When my brother David graduated from Exeter, the boarding school in New Hampshire my parents had sent him to when the war broke out, he came back to England, working his passage as an anti-aircraft gunner on an Indian freighter, and enlisted at Sandhurst. From there he took a commission in the Royal Horse Guards, and saw action in Italy, eventually becoming ADC to the general commanding Number One District in Italy. David's unit reopened the Milan Opera House and he sat in the royal box for the opening night. As his unit came up through Italy he also passed through the village where the family of the 400 Club's head waiter were living. He made a special effort to find them, taking them lots of rations and looking after them as best he could. He never paid another bill in that nightclub for the rest of his life.

My other brother, Alastair, was already at Dartmouth Naval College when the war broke out. He continued his education there and then went into the navy.

One weekend when he was still at school I forwent the attractions of London and the 400 and went down to visit him. It was the end-of-term dance, and my grandmother had given me £20 to take him and his friend out to lunch beforehand at the best hotel in Torquay. We had a bottle of wine and a terrific lunch and the whole thing cost us £2 because during the war, if you had what was on the menu, it was five shillings, everywhere. You could have lunch at Claridge's for five shillings. Mark you, if you had a bread roll it would probably cost you a fiver because it wasn't on the menu. We took the ferry back across from Torquay to Dartmouth and had a lovely time at the dance. Afterwards, my wretched little brother had a guard of honour to see me home – I was staying with the master of rugger and his wife – and I had to kiss the whole lot before I was allowed in. What I didn't know was that the master and his wife were hanging out of the window watching all this. Oh Lord! Anyway, it was rather a nice little adventure.

Alastair didn't really want to go into the navy but he did, all the same, as a regular sailor. His first wartime journey was as a cadet on the HMS *Renown*, which was the vast battleship that took Churchill to America to see Roosevelt. Churchill's daughter, Subaltern Mary Churchill, was on that trip too and when the ship's cat had kittens she was given one for her birthday. I see Mary Churchill still, at the hairdressers.

My dear childhood friend Ronnie Speed from East Kent, who was only a year older than me, and of whom I was terribly fond, was killed at Dunkirk. My favourite cousin, Dick McCall, also a year older than me, joined the Rifle Brigade and was killed at El Alamein. Curiously though, despite friends and cousins dying, I don't remember worrying about my brothers or friends being killed. Perhaps being at Bletchley I was confident the war would be won. Perhaps it is just difficult for a girl in her teens and early twenties to dwell on death.

*

I don't much care about medals and baubles but many people do. At the end of the war, the Wrens who worked in the section next to mine were all given the ordinary War Medal, commonly known as the EOBGO, or Every Other Bugger's Got One. It was just a little ribbon and a round thing. But at least they got something. In my section we were employed by the Foreign Office and we got nothing. After a lot of arguing and annoyance and heavy-weight fuss-making – which I took no part in because I really didn't mind – we were graciously issued with a slightly ridiculous thing that I can only refer to as a badge, which simply says, 'I Also Served'. It made me want to throw up, frankly.

I did, however, lend my strongest support to the campaign to grant a posthumous pardon to Alan Turing, who was convicted of gross indecency, for being homo-sexual, in 1952: a campaign which resulted in Turing being granted a royal pardon by the Queen in December 2013. My mother had a friend called Lady Winifred Renshaw who looked and sounded like the late Queen Mary. I well remember Lady Winifred saying, 'Mr Asquith was a man with whom I would never have travelled alone in a taxi.' ('NSIT' was the rather easily-crackable code my girlfriends and I used back in our Bletchley days: Not Safe In Taxis.) I mentioned this in the House of Lords and repeat it now to make the point that it was not Mr

Asquith's possible behaviour in taxis that is remembered, but what he actually achieved for this country. This country owes Alan Turing a great debt. He was the father of computer science, an extraordinary achievement on its own. But, more than that, the breaking of the German Enigma ciphers using his Bombe machine gave us decisive intelligence in the battle of El Alamein, which was a turning point in the war; it enabled our merchant ships to get past the U-boats, which prevented us from losing the war through starvation; and made a crucial contribution to the success of the D-Day landings.

At the end of the war, Churchill decreed that everything at Bletchley should be destroyed. My colleagues and I have always thought it must be because everything was kept at the end of the First World War, and a book was published, *Room 47*, setting out everything that our intelligence services had done during the war. Well, of course, the Germans read the book from cover to cover. So Churchill certainly wouldn't have wanted the Russians or anyone else to be able to learn how we had done it all. The Bombe machines and Colossus machines – the world's first programmable computers – were taken apart with tweezers and screwdrivers, by the very same Wrens who had operated them probably, and the documentation about their design burnt.

Today Bletchley Park is open to the public and anyone

can visit and see replicas of many of the code-breaking machines. It never looked anything like it looks now (and it certainly never looked anything like it looks in those dreadful films they've made about it – the ones that make it seem like the Americans did everything). There's a new entrance that bears absolutely no relation to what we had: we used to be driven up to just below the front door. The two tennis courts that Churchill was responsible for getting us are now a car park. What they call the lake used to be a dirty little pond. And they've dredged a stone up from the bottom of the pond and put it outside the big house on the grass and said that was where Churchill stood when he came and addressed us all. Well, he didn't at all, he stood on an orange crate. I was there!

Despite all that I would encourage anyone who hasn't done so to visit. What went on at Bletchley Park was hugely important for this country and I would like that fact to be remembered.

CHAPTER SIX

Paris

VE Day was extraordinary. I was still working at Bletchley at the time and we all caught the train up to London and went and stood outside Buckingham Palace and yelled and then we danced all night. Humphrey Lyttelton passed by on the back of an open lorry, playing his trumpet outside Buckingham Palace and down Birdcage Walk, which was heaven. I picked up a lieutenant commander from the navy and spent most of the evening dancing with him. He was a great big chap and we had a marvellous evening – no love in the bushes or anything, it was awfully pure – but I never saw him again. They say that the Royal Princesses, Elizabeth and Margaret, were out on the streets that night too.

For me, who had been sixteen when the war had started, the most wonderful thing was seeing light in London. For nearly six years we had had the blackout and the street lights had been hooded and dimmed. Now London was suddenly full of light. In Piccadilly, there were gas lights with naked flames flickering in beautiful vases. It was time to rejoice, it really was.

After VE Day the work at Bletchley became very boring – or rather even more utterly boring – and I began to desperately wish to get away. It was impossible to leave with the war in Japan still going on, but then I told them that my mother had broken her arm and needed me. That was how I escaped. Actually she had broken her arm, but she didn't need me because she had plenty of help.

Instead, I managed to find myself a job working in Paris for an international organization which had been set up to put the inland transport of Europe back together again: railways, roads, ports and airfields. Paris in 1946, as I'm sure you can imagine, was very special. I had an absolute ball for the two years I was there, doing exactly what I wanted.

It took me twenty-four hours to get from London to Paris. I couldn't go from Dover or Folkestone, I had to go from one of the other smaller ports. And Boulogne didn't exist and Calais had been bombed to hell, so I had to go to Le Havre. The crossing took about six hours. In those days it wasn't at all odd to talk to people on the train or the boat, and during the crossing I got talking to a man who said he had a car coming to fetch him at Le Havre and would I like a lift to Paris. 'You bet,' I said, pleased as anything, but it was pretty silly of me – I didn't know him from Adam. When we got to the port, there was a great big American car waiting for him, which was very unusual. My new friend collected me and put my suitcase in his car and the two of us climbed in and made our way down roads that didn't really exist through a devastated landscape.

We arrived at a little pub – the French equivalent of a pub – and I had my first French meal since my finishing school days. God, it was good. And in the back of the pub I could see all the crew from the ship on which we had come over exchanging packages. I don't know what was in the packages, whether it was illegal drugs, or penicillin – which was highly-prized at that time – or goodness knows what. After this delicious meal I was put back in the expensive car and we continued driving along these hugely pitted roads until we came to a stop in the middle of nowhere. My new friend tooted his horn and a man came running down his drive and again packets were exchanged. Being the inexperienced ass I was, at the time I just thought he was being kind to me. Looking back, I think I must have been the unwitting alibi for some awful Harry Lime-style drugs run. I provided him with a clean passport, so to speak, to get through the port.

We finally arrived in Paris at midnight, whereupon my friend dumped me somewhere and I caught a taxi to my hotel perfectly easily, checked in and went to sleep. The following morning at six o'clock, while I was tucked up in bed, all hell broke loose when the embassy staff went to meet me off the train I should have been on and I wasn't there. I had only just arrived and I was in hot water already. But of course it was all soon sorted out.

When I reported to my office, I was horrified to find out what my job was to be. They had employed me as a registrar because that had been my job title at Bletchley. But being a registrar at Bletchley was a thoroughly peculiar job which didn't conform at all to what might be expected of a registrar in real life, which was – of course – filing. I didn't know what on earth to do with the piles and piles of papers thrust on my desk, or what anybody was talking about. Luckily – bearing in mind that this was an international organization – the boss was English, and he was a nice, gentle man who took a liking to me and changed my job, thank goodness. I could never have done all that filing. Instead, he put me in charge of looking after all the needs of the people who worked in the organization in Paris. I still don't know what the job title was but it was the most heavenly task and I loved it. I found flats for them; I arranged their transport; I organized their parties. All it took was common sense. I had a car and a chauffeur at my disposal, and an office on the fifth floor of a building on the Champs Elysées, above a nightclub

called Mimi Pinson, and I became well known around
Paris because I was spending other people's money on
throwing marvellous parties at the Crillon and the Ritz
and so on.

Since I had no money, but did have this wonderful
job and good connections, my life was a strange mixture
of the really rather squalid and the very very grand.

At first I lived in a rather grotty sort of hotel that
the British Embassy had requisitioned for us all, down
by the Madeleine. I had to take the bus from the hotel
to the office and although at that time my diplomatic
passport meant I could go to the head of the queue,
you can imagine how popular you were if you did that,
so frankly I never did.

After a few weeks, though, I was taken in by an
extremely rich friend of my father who he knew through
the paint business. The friend's name was Monsieur Le
Franc and his daughter, Solange, was about the same age
as me. I think one got tax relief or something if there
was a foreigner living in one's flat, so it was a good solution for everyone. It was a classic Parisian flat, taking up
the whole of one floor of a splendid building (owned in
its entirety by the Le Franc family) at 1 Place d'Alma.
It had an ancient lift – what I would call a French lift,
a sort of cage. And it had those damn lights in the hall-
ways and stairways – the ones where you turn the light

on at the bottom and get in the lift and by the time you get to the top the light had gone off again. I didn't have my own key and I always stayed out too late, and the Le Francs, who had told me I was going out too much and I was to stay in, used to lock the door. So I had to sit on the stairs, getting up and down to turn the damn light on, waiting for the maid to come and let me in. It was exhausting. However, the flat was perfectly lovely, very close to my office on the Champs Elysées, and I absolutely adored it.

My smart new life got even smarter when I started being invited to parties at the British Embassy. At that time our ambassador was Duff Cooper. He and his wife, Lady Diana, the daughter of the Duke of Rutland, were very high-profile and very grand indeed. Duff Cooper had royal connections, had been educated at Eton and Oxford where he had been part of the fashionable set known as the Coterie, and had been a Conservative MP and member of the cabinet in the 1930s, resigning in protest at Chamberlain's policy of appeasement. He was now considered to be a great success in Paris where he was nurturing a reputation for gambling, drinking and womanizing. Lady Diana had also been active in the Coterie and, after many of their mutual friends had been killed in the Great War, she had married Duff, rather to her parents' consternation, as though clever and ambitious he had no money to speak of. She had been on the stage, too, playing the Madonna in Max Reinhardt's play *The Miracle* in London and on Broadway, and she was generally considered to be the great beauty of her time. Ernie Bevin, the socialist foreign secretary, was crazy about her, despite her being an aristocratic society hostess and his being a socialist.

The Coopers' social secretary was a rather camp chap who of course became a great friend of mine, and soon made sure I was invited to all the embassy parties. It certainly wouldn't have happened otherwise, I'm sure – I wasn't on a social par with the Coopers.

Apart from the gorgeous flat and the lovely parties, I continued in my role of useful alibi for my father and for various other people, which meant some nice meals and some rather nice things, too. One friend of my mother's who had a boyfriend in Paris used to come over and say she was taking me out. It was such a lie, she barely ever came near me, but she told me what she was doing and treated me to the odd dinner because she owed me. And then my father's beautiful girlfriend, the former Ziegfeld Girl who had married the terrible rotten landlord, decided to buy me a suit from the great French couturier Lucien Lelong. So off I went and chose a suit. The models walked up and down in front of you and you picked out the one you liked best, then it was made to measure. I can remember it very well because I am always amazed at my choice, it was so hideous. It was green with a thin red stripe. Ghastly. And I had a cheap little hat to go with it. But even worse, perhaps, is the fact that I accepted such an expensive gift from my father's girlfriend. Still, unlike the Lelong outfits I had inherited from my petite friend Miss Baron as a child, it did fit me beautifully.

There was rationing in Paris just as there was in London, of course, but their idea of rationing was ludicrous compared to ours. My flatmate Solange married in 1946, in the most magnificent, flowing dress with an enormous train that would have used up several years' clothing coupons in the UK. And it never seemed to me to be terribly difficult to get hold of food: you could get anything. Mind you, I do remember once being at a posh wedding where the food was just delicious, and I sort of eased forward towards a table heaving with mouth-watering delicacies and the woman in front of me, elegant as they come, with beautiful blue-white hair and a delicate hat, turned round to me and said, in French, 'Don't push in Madame, I've got eclairs in both pockets.'

I made friends easily: through work, through the embassy parties and through the tennis club. Although all hope of junior Wimbledon had faded with the war – I was too old now – I still played and I met a lot of French people that way. There were also various people I had known at Bletchley in Paris, including one or two who had been very kind to me and continued to be kind to me, but who were now married, so I had to be rather careful.

I went out with various chaps while I was there. There was always a fellow in tow – Paris was very lively, with plenty of people passing in and out on some business or other because of all the rebuilding and diplomatic work going on: Brits, Americans, every nationality you can think of except for Germans. I don't remember ever seeing a German. But I suppose that's not entirely surprising.

But I have to say honestly that of all the delightful men I met there the only one I really loved was a man I shall refer to as the American. And eventually – although not for many years – I came to understand that he didn't love me. He loved me as a friend, yes, but not as anything else. I met the American through cousins of his who asked me to dinner. Our sense of humour was the same and we spent the evening screaming with laughter. We were immediately firm friends, alas; because almost as immediately I was desperately in love with him.

The American was a fine figure of a man, and terribly rich, the son of an old American family, and of course he had been very brave during the war. He had been dropped by parachute into France and fought with the Maquis behind enemy lines. One weekend he took me on a journey through the Vercors mountains, showing me all the places where he had fought alongside them: the Maquis hospital buried in the mountains that had been attacked by the Germans; the little town in the Dauphiné where the Maquis had ambushed a German convoy of trucks carrying radar equipment in August 1944; a house in which he had been trapped. He took me to a village where everybody – babies and old age pensioners, everybody – had been killed by the Nazis. The whole village. It was fascinating and I saw things that I don't suppose exist any more. Another weekend he took me to meet his cousins in the South of France, who were the people Mrs Simpson went to when she did a runner. They were frightfully intimidating and so were their other guests. There was some kind of French duchess, and Nancy Mitford: I was thrilled to meet her but ever so scared of her. She was the kind of person who would take you up on every little remark and make you think you had got it wrong – and you probably had. And then, because you were frightened, you did it again. One of my earrings dropped into the soup. I was utterly mortified but she thought it was hilarious.

Several of my dear friends were much more successful than me romantically and these post-war years were studded with weddings, many of which were great society occasions, preceded by lavish engagement parties and followed soon after by equally lavish christenings.

My Bletchley friend Sally was the first: she married Bill Astor in June 1945, a month after they had first met at a cocktail party on VE Day. He was a parliamentary candidate and needed a wife, and she was an ex-deb with time passing her by. But it wasn't until 1951 that Sally managed to produce an heir, which was all-important to the Astors – Bill would succeed his father as 3rd Viscount Astor in 1952. Poor Sally had miscarriage after miscarriage and then finally stayed in bed for seven months at Bletchington Park in order to give birth to William. While she was stuck in bed for all those months I used to go down there most weekends to keep her company. But despite William's arrival, Sally and Bill were divorced soon after, in 1953, and Sally married Thomas Baring, a lieutenant colonel in the Derbyshire Yeomanry. Despite the fact that they both remarried, I think Bill always loved her. Certainly he used to say that in the eyes of God he was still married to Sally. In fact, he used to say it when his third wife, Bronwen, was at the other end of the table, which wasn't exactly tactful.

In December 1946 the other half of the pair from Bletchley, my great friend Osla, married John Henniker-Major, who had no money but was heir to the 7th Baron Henniker, a 95-room house and a 2,000-acre estate. They proceeded quickly to have two sons and a daughter. John had served in North Africa and Yugoslavia, where he worked with a distinguished group of officers that included Bill Deakin, Randolph Churchill and Evelyn Waugh, trying to make contact with Tito. After the war he returned to a glittering career in the Foreign Office, rising to become ambassador to Jordan and then Denmark. I don't think Osla was very good at being Madam Ambassador because she was so spoilt and no one quite realized it until she had to do things that she didn't want to do. On the other hand, the King of Jordan's mother adored her, and showered her with turquoises, so she must have done something right.

Poor Osla died much too young, in 1974, having been ill for years. I spoke at her memorial service, and the man sitting next to me had been crazy about Oz, and was so furious he hadn't been asked to speak that he sat there hating me all the way through. I was longing for a kind word – just a 'well done' – and he said nothing. It was quite difficult.

*

After I had been in Paris for nearly two years I was invited to go on holiday with some of my friends from the tennis club. We stayed in Quiberon in Brittany, in a hotel on the beach; the hotel was staffed by German ex-prisoners of war and there were terrible complications with water and the loos. All my French tennis friends were married and there was a big group of couples. I had no boyfriend at the time so I was there on my own. The day I arrived everyone met on the beach and they took all their clothes off – everything. I was deeply shocked but felt I had to do the same so I took everything off, too, terribly embarrassed, and ran down the beach into the water. When I came back they had hidden my clothes. I ran up and down that sodding beach, stark naked, with them all laughing at me. I never did that again.

After that tricky start I did have the most wonderful holiday, eating wonderful seafood, including lots of *araignées de mer*, or spider crabs, which are better than lobster and utterly marvellous: I don't understand why we don't eat them in Britain. I don't remember what if anything I paid for that holiday, perhaps I didn't pay at all and was the guest of one of my friends. But nothing in life is ever free. When I came back to Paris I stayed with one of the couples. On our first night back, I was fast asleep and in came the husband, saying, 'You're not my ward any more, you're grown-up enough,' and leaping into my bed. I fought him off. It was quite a tussle, I can tell you, sheer fisticuffs, and all conducted in whispers because his wife was there in the flat somewhere, asleep. Afterwards, he was sure I was going to tell. I didn't of course – his poor wife would have been furious. But it was deeply unpleasant and I decided it was high time I went back to England.

CHAPTER SEVEN

London

After I returned to London, in the late summer of 1948, I stayed initially with my friend Sue Graham (who had been Sue Surtees when I first knew her at Bletchley) in her flat on Pont Street, just behind Harrods.

I'd stayed there with Sue during my Paris years whenever I was back in London. It wasn't really a flat, it was the whole of the fourth floor of a vast townhouse. Sue's brother, John Surtees, who was a wine merchant, often stayed too. He had been a prisoner of war since Calais fell – since right at the beginning of the war in other words – and it had affected him deeply. He couldn't ever bear for a door to be shut, and he used to cut the bread very very carefully, to make sure that every slice was exactly the same size. In 1942 Sue had married Charles Graham, the heir to a baronetcy in Cumberland. When Sue became pregnant at the end of 1945 it was feared that she would miscarry. Charles was still away with the

Scots Guards at the time, so I took my annual leave from my job in Paris to look after her. Happily, in August 1946 her son James was safely delivered and I was invited to become his godmother.

But now that I needed a permanent place to live I couldn't stay with Sue and Charles and baby James forever. It was 'I don't know what to do with Jean' time again. As it happened, around that time an American company that had been bust since the Great Depression suddenly took wings and paid out on the large quantities of stock my mother was still holding. For years and years these shares had been worthless but now suddenly my parents had money again. My mother persuaded my father that they should use some of it to buy me a flat in London. She also bought an ill-fated farm called Bull Town for my father, which I hated. She sank most of the rest of the money into a succession of houses that she bought, did up and sold again.

The first of these was Digges Court, in Westwell near Charing: an early eighteenth-century house that was very badly placed, with a road right in front and a hill behind. But my mother saw the possibilities and she went crazy about it. She put six bathrooms into that house. 'Well, every bedroom should have a bathroom,' she said. That might be how they build houses now but it was certainly not how houses were built then. Then it was Lympne Hall, Hope Farm, and so on and on.

Bull Town itself was a horrid mouldy little house but my mother made it look beautiful. That was her genius. She also converted a ruined old granary on the farm into cottages and, to make my father happy, spent £3,000 on buying a bull called Blushing Liberator. (The first house I bought with my husband several years later cost £800.) That bloody bull was 3,000 quid down the drain. He died without ever having sired anything. My parents had a lot of fun with the houses and their farming, but after their fun, the money had all gone.

My flat was on Grosvenor Crescent Mews and it was simply heavenly. The mews was just west of Hyde Park Corner, behind what was then St George's Hospital and is now the Lanesborough Hotel. The flat was on the first floor, up a steep staircase, and had three bedrooms, and my friends Pempe Crossley and Mary Cobb soon moved in to share it with me. If we opened the hall window we could look out onto the mews, which was still then used for stabling horses. It was a very unusual flat.

Pempe and Mary were both terrific fun and both rather naughty. Pempe, whose father was Anthony Crossley the MP, at one point worked for a trainer at Newmarket and rode out for him in the mornings. You have to be very good to do that. So Pempe loved having the horses in the

1. My father in his uniform as a Bengal Lancer.

2. My parents skiing at St Moritz on their honeymoon.

3. With my mother.

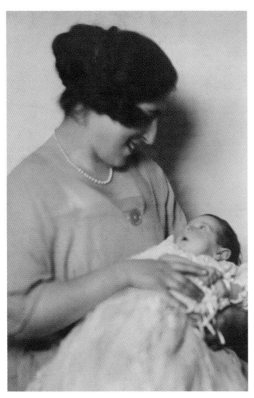

4. The drawing room at Rowling.

5. Young Jean.

6. With Mademoiselle Arbel and Mademoiselle Dettelbach at Montrichard.

7. In Paris, 1939.

8. With Lloyd George, on his farm at Churt.

9. Robin Carey-Evans. 10. Osla Benning.

11. On the way to Henry and Shirley Paget's wedding. Left to right: Sally Astor, Diana Lyttelton, Osla Henniker-Major, me, 1948.

12. On holiday in Quiberon, 1946.

13. The Opera Ball, March 1950. The theme was clearly
Wagnerian, though my dear friend and boss Lord Hinchingbrooke, is
sporting a Roman tunic beneath his Germanic helmet and beard.
I'm on the far left, clearly dressed as Brünnhilde.

14. Hinch and his vast family.

15. My brother David's engagement party at the Cavalry Club.
Left to right: my father, me, Alastair, my mother, Amy and David,
October 1951.

16. Skiing with the American, L'Eclose, Alpe d'Huez, 1951.

17. In the south of France with the American (*right*), 1951.

18. In my office at Fletcher D. Richards Inc.

19. A typical New York party, Greenwich Village, 1953.
I'm in the middle of the back row.

mews too – except when one boyfriend turned out to be allergic and so could never come to visit her. Anyway that boyfriend didn't marry her. She married the first of her three husbands, another great friend, Ronnie Callendar, in 1951. Mary – whose father was also an MP, known as Foot to his family because he had lost a foot in the war – married a tea planter from Ceylon.

*

I had a succession of jobs, starting, inauspiciously, with a job my father found for me at Peter Jones. Of all unsuitable things I was put in the department where schoolgirls' outfitting was arranged. I didn't find it very thrilling. Every day a girl used to come to the office at the back of the department and sign for something, I didn't know what, and I didn't take much notice. Then she'd leave. That was as exciting as it got. One day, after I had been doing this dreadful job for about six months, I was called by my boss and another man into the office, where I was stood in front of a desk and accused of stealing clothing coupons. Rationing was still in force, and evidently a lot of clothing coupons had gone missing. I had no idea what they were talking about, and said so, before being sent out of the room and left in a corridor. I didn't know what to do. I couldn't think how I could possibly convince them that I hadn't stolen the coupons: it didn't seem to be the kind of thing one could prove. So I sat in the loo for quite a long time, and then I rang up my father and told him what had happened. He said I was to come straight out of there, which is what I did.

In the end, they discovered that the wretched girl who had kept coming and signing for things had pinched them. Apparently, she'd been signing for the clothing coupons and pocketing them. Once they worked that out, they offered me my job back. That job, or any job I wanted. I said, 'Fuck the lot of you.' I never went back.

That wasn't the last time I told Peter Jones to go to hell. There's a second-hand jewellery counter in the jewellery department on the first floor of Peter Jones. You get out of the lift and it's right in front of you. I have bought a lot of jewellery from there: they don't always know what they are selling and sometimes one can find some jolly good things. Once, when I was a minister, I had bought earrings in Egypt and Peter Jones had a necklace on the second-hand counter that matched them, which I bought. I then decided that it was over-priced and I sent it back, but they refused to take it. So I invited the directors of Peter Jones to tea at the House of Lords – you know, that's a lovely weapon to have up your sleeve – and before they arrived I made sure that I had the key to one of the two interview rooms and in that interview room I laid out all the jewellery I had ever bought from them. After tea, I took them in there. I really don't know to this day what they thought of the whole thing, but I got my money back.

Quite recently I also experienced the most enormous kindness at the hands of Peter Jones. They have a hat department, quite small, which had a very nice woman working there who always understood exactly the way my mind works. I was there choosing a hat – in fact I made this lovely lady make the final choice – and as I left, it was raining very hard. I had never seen such rain, it was just awful. This kind lady insisted on coming down with me, without a coat or anything, and then she took my bag with the hat in it and told me to queue for a taxi. And so I did. And in Sloane Square, in the rain, there was quite a queue. But when I was still quite a long way from the front of the queue, a taxi pulled up and she was in it. She had gone off with my hat, found a taxi and brought it back to the rank for me. She just pushed me in, pushed herself out, and that was that. Well, afterwards I of course wrote to the directors to say that I have never had such incredible service, such kindness and help. They replied, very pleased, and the next time I went to Peter Jones I took their letter with me to show her, but maddeningly she wasn't there any more. I left it for her and I just pray she got it. It was so lovely to be looked after so well by a complete stranger. But isn't it curious how

I seem to have had both the best and the worst service from the same shop – both as a member of staff and as a customer.

After I told Peter Jones to go to hell that first time, I went to work for Viscount Hinchingbrooke, then a Conservative MP. I can't remember how I got into that – perhaps I saw an advertisement. Anyway, I applied for the job and was interviewed while sitting on a bench in the corridor of Central Lobby in the Commons. I was delighted that I got it. I used to cycle from my flat at Hyde Park Corner to my little office on the top floor of 17 Great College Street – a dear little house on a pretty street just behind Westminster Abbey. And, you know, it was an extraordinary job, because Hinch – I always knew him as Hinch – was frightfully *dégagé* as a boss. When I first arrived, he said, 'Oh, the files are in the cabinet, just go through them and read what you want.' The first file I picked up was all his correspondence with his wife, Rosie, at the time of their engagement! They had seven children and were a frightfully good-looking pair: he was six foot six with long long legs and just beautiful. She was blonde, buxom and terribly alive.

I used to take dictation for Hinch, and type up the letters in my little turret. But after a while he gave up and just let me write the letters, because I did better on my own than trying to take dictation with my dreadful shorthand. Sometimes he would say, 'My God, this is a very good letter.' Not often, but enough to be rather pleasing. When I had done all the letters I would drop them round at the House of Commons for him to sign. Sometimes I would go in and listen to the debates going on, sometimes I didn't. Once when I was walking through the House with Hinch, Winston Churchill stopped him in the corridor. It was the only time I met Churchill. He said to Hinch, 'If you stop this damned nonsense, you have a future. If you don't, you have none.' The nonsense being that Hinch was very anti-Europe, although he would have said he was simply very pro-Empire. But despite Churchill's admonition, Hinch went right back into the chamber and carried on arguing against Europe. I am sure it did him no good: his political career ended in a very sad way. He was able to be an MP as Lord Hinchingbrooke because he wasn't a real lord. It was simply an honorary title as he was the heir to the Earl of Sandwich. When his father died in 1962 he became the 10th Earl of Sandwich and, as a peer, automatically lost his seat in the Commons. After the passage of the Peerages Act in 1963, Hinch disclaimed his peerage so that he could return to the Commons, but he was never able to win another seat. When I became a peer myself I had him to tea in the House of Lords and he did look wistful as person after person came up and called him Hinch (even though he was plain Victor Montagu by then) and said how lovely it was to see him. I'm sure that if he hadn't been so stupidly outspoken against Europe things might have turned out differently for him.

Sally Astor, my old friend from Bletchley whose husband Bill had been an MP, gave me a lot of help in gatecrashing the Commons secretarial scene. All of Lloyd George's political staff whom I had got to know at Churt during the war were back at the House too, working away for his daughter Megan Lloyd George who was now an MP. But although it was lovely to know people, I wasn't ever entirely part of the secretaries' gang, and didn't really want to be, because I knew Hinch and a lot of other MPs and high-profile people socially.

The weddings continued apace. My friends Hugh Rock-savage and Lavinia Leslie got married at Cholmondeley, in Cheshire, just one of his family's great houses, the other being Houghton Hall in Norfolk. Hugh's father was the Marquess of Cholmondeley, his mother Sybil was a Sassoon and his maternal grandmother a Rothschild; they were so grand they were practically royalty. Lavinia, however, was a perfectly ordinary girl but she certainly married into quite an extraordinary life. She and Hugh inherited Cholmondeley when the old marquess died and she still lives there today. It is vast, and a very castle-y castle, with turrets and so on. They both longed for a boy, but Lavinia produced girl after girl. When she eventually produced an heir, in 1960, she told me that she lay in her bed at Cholmondeley and she could see that on every hilltop a fire had been lit in celebration. When it was the son's turn to produce an heir, he found a girl who brilliantly produced twin boys straight away.

In 1948 my friend Shirley Morgan, the daughter of the celebrated novelists Charles Morgan and Hilda Vaughan, married Henry Paget, becoming the Marchioness of Anglesey. Henry's family owned most of Anglesey and lived on the island at Plas Newydd, where his father, the 6th Marquess, had commissioned Rex Whistler to paint the most wonderful murals all the way round the dining room. There was also a most marvellous boot at Plas Newydd, dating back to the Battle of Waterloo. The 1st Marquess was a great hero of that battle, in which he lost his leg. The story went that he was riding next to the Duke of Wellington when he was shot. 'My God, sir, I've lost a leg,' said the marquess. Reply from the duke: 'My God, sir, and so you have.' They kept the leg and the boot. I don't know what happened to the leg, but the boot was certainly at Anglesey. Henry, who had had a big walk-out with Sally before she married Bill Astor, was extremely eccentric. I particularly remember him on his feet in the front row of the Empire Cinema in Leicester Square, shouting and waving his arms about, attempting to conduct the organ.

In 1950 came the wedding of my friends Patrick Telfer-Smollett and Gina Fox. Patrick was in the Scots Guards. Hardly anyone knows this now but the Guards had provided a nightly picquet to guard the Bank of England since it had been attacked during the Gordon Riots in 1780 – a tradition that continued until the 1970s. Each night two guardsmen would march up there and then, since the Bank of England doesn't tend to get attacked, they would get terribly bored. Patrick was often a member of the picquet and a gang of his friends, including me, used to go there and play strip poker to help them pass the time.

I also spent many memorable weekends through these years with my 'set' at Bletchington Park, where the Astors were hosts, or Cholmondeley, Combermere Abbey (my friends the Crossleys' house in Shropshire) or on the island of Jura (the Astors again). Once I holidayed in Cannes on board the *Semita*, a beautiful yacht that was put at our disposal. Another time – or perhaps the same time – I stayed again at Eden Roc, the scene of my humiliation at the hands of my mother in a boy's bathing costume. This time I chose my own bathing costume, and I looked rather good in it. I seem to remember I was sent on that holiday with the laughable idea that I would be a good influence on one of the other girls. She was very wild and naughty indeed, so perhaps I was. Though I rather doubt it.

I often went to Hinchingbrooke itself, to stay with Hinch and his family. Hinchingbrooke, in Cambridgeshire, was a very big and very grand old house with beautiful gardens. It had been in Hinch's family since Sir Sydney Montagu had bought it from Oliver Cromwell (not the Lord Protector, but his uncle) in 1627. It featured heavily in the diaries of Samuel Pepys, who worked as a secretary at Hinchingbrooke, and it quite literally had skeletons in its closets: one day nuns' bones were found in the cupboard under the stairs. It's a school now, having been sold by Hinch when he relinquished his title.

Whenever Hinch's children came to stay in London, I would be detailed to take them out. Trying to look after that many children is extremely difficult. We usually went to the Tower of London but what they really enjoyed was going up and down on the escalators in the Underground: they weren't the least bit interested in anything else.

One night Hinch and six or seven others came to dinner with me in my mews flat before we all went on to the opera ball. We were all in the most extravagant fancy dress: I remember Hinch's valet later saying to me, 'My dear, it took me two weeks to get his sheets clean,' because Hinch was wearing a Roman tunic and had browned his legs. Afterwards we went on to the 400 and I ended up dancing with a Roman gladiator. It was a typically glamorous evening but I remember it more clearly than some of the others because the following day the Roman gladiator came into my office at 17 Great College Street, walked up and down, up and down, and then went off to the Cavalry Club on Piccadilly, found a gun, went to a room and shot himself. I've always felt I was to blame – I've never known why he did it, but I should have listened to him more carefully and noticed that something was badly wrong. It was sixty years ago but I still think about it.

It was my father who told me. He was chairman of the Cavalry Club by then, which was a great honour for him, but also a lot of work and certainly a lot of drinking. It was also my father who broke the news that I had got the sack from working for Hinch. I didn't get the sack exactly, but they were going to move me out of London to work at Hinchingbrooke House, which I didn't want to do. My father took me out to dinner to tell me. But of course, having said no thank you to working at Hinchingbrooke I missed the job terribly and was miserable.

My third job was as secretary to the chairman of the United Service Club. The Club was on Pall Mall, just off Trafalgar Square and opposite the Athenaeum in a wonderful Nash building (now part of the Institute of Directors). I had to type out the menus every day, and – typical me, I couldn't leave well enough alone – I organized ping-pong tournaments between the valets and the kitchen staff. I can't remember much else about what exactly I did there, but I do know I loved it.

*

Along with my succession of jobs came a succession of chaps. I was still terribly pure – I was so good at taking avoiding action, following my excellent training with French men, that I became known as 'Mademoiselle Ne Me Touchez Pas'. But I always had some chap or other on the go.

One friend of my father's, whom I later discovered had already had an affair with his daughter's best friend, had a good try at having an affair with me one night. Boy oh boy, he did not get very far. But I was much too cowardly to come out with it and tell him no. Instead, I just dropped him off at my father's club – he got out of the cab and I simply stayed in it as it pulled away – left him with my father, and then didn't go home for hours.

While all these boyfriends, whether suitable or decidedly unsuitable, were coming and going I was, of course, still madly in love with the American. And the American and I, always accompanied by one or other of his friends, continued to have constant adventures and a hell of a lot of fun.

In the summers we holidayed together in France or

Spain. In 1949, I drove down on my own (very brave) and met the American and his friend near Cassis. We spent our days at the beach, and it was idyllic. Except for the dreadful day I nearly drowned. We had set up our camp for the day on a very beautiful rocky bit of the coast, with no beach, and I had jumped into the sea and swum about a bit, and I found that I couldn't get back to dry land. There was an undertow that kept dragging me back into the sea. I tried saying 'Help', but they didn't hear me. Then I shouted, 'Help!' but they just looked up, laughed, and went on with their conversation. By the time I finally managed to get out of the water on my own, what felt like hours later, though it can only have been minutes, I really thought I might have died.

In 1950 the highlight of our trip was a visit to the *corrida* or bullfight in Aix-en-Provence. It wasn't really my thing, because I cared dreadfully about the poor horses in particular, but I wasn't going to admit it because I was so keen on the American. And then, of course, I found that I did get rather caught up in the whole thing. The *picadores* on horseback and *banderilleros* with their capes and rather dashing matadors paraded in front of us in their splendid costumes, accompanied by stirring music – pasa dobles played by a live band. And then the famous Jesús Gracia Pina went into action. It was tremendously exciting. The following year we went one better – going to Pamplona for the *encierro*, or running of the bulls, which is the most astonishing sight. An American girl called Jackie Bouvier was there too, with her sister, and she managed to start a fight. Jackie was drinking wine out of the traditional animal skin and spilt some down her white blouse, which proceeded to go transparent. Someone said something rude about her bosom, someone else said, 'How dare you,' and a big fight broke out. That was the end of her bull fighting: she left and never went back.

Sadly, she had not made such a striking impression on my brother Alastair earlier that year – a failure on his part that he was desperately upset about for the rest of his life. Alastair was back in London on leave from the navy with some of his able-bodied seamen friends (he had stayed in the navy after the war, where he had served as ADC to the Governor General of New Zealand). Alastair and his friends had agreed to serve as bartender and waiters at a drinks party I was throwing. I had met Jackie on my rounds and thought she was awfully pretty and thought, too, that Alastair might rather like her. After everyone had gone I said to my brother, 'Did you make a date with her?' and he said, 'No, she had dry hair.' My foolish brother had turned down a date with Jacqueline Bouvier, who later became Jackie Kennedy.

After Pamplona, it was back to France for me, for more bull fighting (Arles and Marseilles) and sunbathing. Marseilles was a very disappointing affair, held in a football stadium and ruined by a lack of atmosphere and a very bad mistral. Arles, however, was spectacular: the Roman amphitheatre that had once played host to gladiatorial contests and chariot races was completely full of people young and old yelling and cheering at the tops of their voices.

Over Christmas 1951, the American, his friend Bob Storer and I went skiing in Alpe d'Huez in the French Alps. It was very brave of me because I had never skied before in my life but it is amazing what one will do to impress a boyfriend. I was still working at the United Service Club in St James' at the time, and the valets there lent me what they called 'deceased officers' effects' – in other words, great long underwear with flaps that buttoned at the bum, left behind by ancient generals – to wear on the slopes. They were very warm but not exactly flattering, and I spent a lot of time ensuring that the American should not see me in my elderly generals' underpants.

My enduring memory of that holiday is my ski instructor saying to me, in a terrible English accent, but with admirable sang-froid, 'Ze water iz rising.' I was sitting on him in a stream – no doubt as the result of some kind of skiing calamity caused by me. I did love skiing, but I was so very bad at it.

But once the holiday was over, in January 1952, I set off on my next big adventure. And this time I was on my own.

CHAPTER EIGHT

New York

My mother and everyone on her side of the family was American, and my brother David had lived in the United States with our American cousins since he had been sent there as a boy. I had never felt myself to be American in any way, but I had always longed to go there.

After the end of the war, in which he had served with distinction, David had returned to the States and made a life for himself there. He was supposed to become the chairman of the family paint company in Chicago – and he could have done, it was all agreed – but he decided it wasn't what he wanted. So he quit the paint company and took himself from Chicago to New York, where he got himself a job as an elevator boy in Saks Fifth Avenue. He had no money, and developed alopecia with the stress of it. But even with the alopecia, he was, at six foot five, both very tall and very attractive and he found himself in great demand. He seemed to have inherited our father's ability to devastate any woman he cast eyes on with just a raised eyebrow and twinkling smile. And going up and down in the lift all day he met all kinds of people. One day he met a girl who worked at J. Walter Thompson, the advertising agency, and this girl got him a job there as a messenger. He went in at the bottom but he certainly rose fast. By the time I was heading out to New York, in 1952, David was a name to conjure with in New York advertising and married to the scion of a fine American family.

He had chosen a shy, pretty girl called Amy Robinson, the sheltered daughter of a well-known Connecticut lawyer. Amy had never really been out in the world at all but after their wedding in Hartford, Connecticut, in October 1951 they came to London, where my parents threw them a great cocktail party and dinner at the Cavalry Club. Sadly for me, as it meant that David wouldn't actually be in New York to look after me, they had then flown on to Rome, where David had a new assignment. But although David wasn't going to be there, lots of his old girlfriends were – including the original girl in the Saks lift, Patsy Shepherd.

So, all alone, I left London for America on board the RMS *Mauretania*, a huge ocean liner. I was travelling steerage, with all my things packed into my grandmother's old cabin trunk. This was an old-fashioned wooden trunk with reinforced corners and embossed initials, designed for wealthy passengers with armies of servants to carry the damn thing. It was huge and enormously heavy and not at all suitable for a young woman travelling on her own, but my mother thought it was and so I was sent off with it.

My awful trunk barely fitted into my cabin, so it was lucky that I found I was sharing it with the ship's tart – she was barely ever there at the same time as me. I only went there to sleep, at night, and she only went there to sleep, during the day. We would pass in the morning, when she would waft in as I was getting up, and say, 'My dear, I've had such a time!' I was deeply shocked because, despite the odd *amour*, I was not at all sophisticated. My mother would have been horrified. The other passenger I particularly remember was a young student called Shirley Brittain Catlin (later Shirley Williams, now Baroness Williams). She was very intellectual and serious and made me feel rather flighty. Our friendship did not bloom.

I arrived in New York six days later, on 28 January 1952, feeling terribly brave. Patsy Shepherd and a couple of David's other girlfriends – none of whom I had ever met before – were there to meet me. Patsy was a terribly attractive, very sophisticated and rather naughty redhead who I rather think always longed to marry my brother. The idiot had gone to his wedding and cried loudly all the way through. But she was always terribly kind to David and then in turn frightfully good to me. I was well aware it was all really for David, which was embarrassing in a way, and yet I didn't ever feel embarrassed because she was so much fun.

Patsy had found me somewhere to stay, in a sort of flat above the famous Stork Club on East 53rd Street, just east of Fifth Avenue. So off we went. The Stork Club was famously glamorous but my fourth-floor flat above it was not. Patsy and I wrestled my wretched cabin trunk up four flights of terribly narrow stairs, to discover a tiny room that already had three beds in it and almost no room at all for anything else. You can imagine how much love I felt for my cabin trunk at that moment.

But having arrived in New York with £2 in my pocket, I couldn't afford anything else. After a few weeks, though, I moved to a better flat on East 81st Street. I was always poor during those New York years, but the first two weeks were the worst. In those days one couldn't bring money out of the UK easily, and, although I had a job, I wouldn't be paid for a fortnight. I couldn't even afford to eat. It hadn't occurred to me – nor clearly to my parents or to any of my brother's friends – what a predicament I would be in. And now that I was in it, I didn't want to tell anyone. All my brother's friends threw cocktail parties for me – lovely drinks parties with great bowls full of potato crisps – and I didn't meet a soul at them because I was so hungry all the time that all I did was wolf down the crisps. Round and round I went, party after party, stuffing the crisps into my mouth.

My brother had found me my job, at an advertising agency called Fletcher D. Richards, based in the Rockefeller Plaza, between 49th and 50th streets on Fifth Avenue. (Rather boringly, though I suppose I can see why, David's own company, J. Walter Thompson, didn't like to employ two members of the same family.) It couldn't have been anywhere grander but I'm afraid I wasn't a bit interested in the work – I was only interested in having a good time in New York – and I did a truly terrible job.

Even after I started getting paid, I still felt poor. I used to go through the bins outside the back of the Stork Club and find handbags and all sorts of lovely things, which I kept. I got my wardrobe from shops on Sixteenth Avenue, where on a Friday they sold slightly imperfect designer clothes for nearly nothing. I found some extra-ordinary things there. Once, when I went into a call box to telephone a friend, the machine broke and showered me with money. I stayed there counting the nickels and dimes for a good half an hour, completely emptying the thing. Afterwards, my bag weighed a ton, but I was rich for once.

But of course although I had no money I had rich

friends and relations, so evenings were spent at the swankiest places in New York, and weekends continued to be spent away at one country house or another, and for the next two years I had the most marvellous time.

One of the first friends I made was a man called Riv Winant, an American who had fought at the Battle of Okinawa with the Marine Corps during the war and then studied at Balliol College, Oxford. Riv's father, John Winant, had been the American ambassador to the UK during the war and – unlike his predecessor, Joseph Kennedy – had been a very good ambassador. Joseph Kennedy had been so pro-appeasement he was practically a Nazi sympathizer but when Riv's father arrived in 1941, when we were in the middle of the Battle of Britain and the Blitz, he said, 'I'm very glad to be here. There's no place I'd rather be at this time than in England.' John Winant looked like Abraham Lincoln – wonderful, in other words. But Riv looked like Micky Rooney and was therefore on the small side. We did not go well together, he and I. But he was a friend of David's, and he appeared the day after I arrived in New York and said he would take me out to dinner. At the restaurant, he ordered me a dry martini. I had never had a dry martini. So I had my dry martini, and then I had another one. And then of course I was drunk. I said, 'Excuse me,' and then went out into the street, which was covered in thick snow, hailed a taxi, got back to my flat above the Stork Club, took all my clothes off and had a shower. Then I put my clothes back on, headed back downstairs and got back into another taxi. I said, 'Could you please take me to a restaurant with a tree behind it?' Well, practically every street in New York has trees and I don't know how the taxi driver found it but he did. The waiters were all out in the snow looking for me. It was awful! They thought I was dead.

Riv never made a pass at me, but we became great friends and he was very good to me. On my first New York birthday he organized a cocktail party for seventy of my greatest friends. We also spent a lot of weekends together at his mother's house on Long Island. The house was right by the water, and had obviously had a hell of a lot of money spent on it. It was all done up beautifully in a 1930s style. Because he was so rich, there were always lots of people hanging round Riv. They were all pretty awful and I didn't like them much.

Soon after that first martini, I ate my first American pudding, which was such an event that I took a photograph of it. (In those days, unlike today, one didn't tend to take photographs of one's pudding.) It was at the Round Hill Country Club in Greenwich, Connecticut, and it was chocolate cake covered with chocolate ice cream covered with marshmallow sauce covered with chocolate sauce. There had been nothing like that in England for years. It was delicious.

Patsy Shepherd introduced me to the River Club, which was very English in atmosphere, but also very laid back, and not swanky at all, with tennis courts and swimming baths. We played a lot of tennis there because Patsy was a damn good tennis player. But she also very kindly let me use her membership to entertain the American – with whom I was still madly in love – when he came over from Paris. Lunch was laid on for me and I could welcome him there as though I was a member, and not have to pay for anything in front of him. It was jolly good of her.

My sister-in-law's family had a lovely house in East Hampton, on the south shore of Long Island in a very swell location by the sea. You were either in or you were out at those Long Island resorts, and Amy's family was definitely in. We ate and swam at their club, the Maidstone Club, and sunbathed on its private beach. America at that time really was the most undemocratic country; the beach in East Hampton was strictly for the upper class members of the private clubs only – no blacks, no ordinary people, other than on a tiny strip right at the end. And it was the same right through the United States.

Amy was one of four sisters and when they were all there, chattering away nineteen to the dozen, their poor father used to go quietly mad. One day they had littered the floor of their drawing room with gramophone records and he just walked over the whole lot and smashed them into bits. With resulting hysterics. I spent many happy weekends with the Robinsons in East Hampton and made lots of friends, including the poshest doctor in New York.

I was on the private beach at the club one day, when Dr Neergaard, who was an East Hampton neighbour of the Robinsons, turned to me and said, 'I can never remember your name. What is it?' Lord knows why, but I told him, 'It's Shufflebottom.' It obviously tickled him that someone in such a swell spot would say such a thing because from then on I had a tame, madly expensive Fifth Avenue doctor, for whom I never queued and I never paid a thing. All the tennis I had played as a child had ruined my back so I must have seen him dozens of times. No matter how long the queue in his waiting room was, nor how grand the patients waiting might be – and they were usually very grand, because he was the most fashionable doctor in New York – he'd always come out and say, 'Come in Miss Shufflebottom,' and in I would go. I jumped the smartest queues because dear Dr Neergaard knew who I was. He was my father's age I suppose, and it wasn't anything naughty: he simply loved my sense of humour and hearing all my gossip and what I was up to with my young men. When I left to go back to England I said, 'Honestly, Dr Neergaard, I really must pay you something.'

He said 'Would $10 be too much?' Wasn't that adorable?

The Robinsons not only introduced me to Dr Neergaard and the Hamptons, but they also invited me to spend my first American Christmas at their family home in Hartford, where Amy and David had got married. It was a wonderful Christmas – I received a great many goodies, which pleased me more than somewhat, and we played a splendid new game called Scrabble.

My first New York New Year's Eve was quite a different cup of tea. I went to a party given by a friend, which was perfectly pleasant but not exhilarating. At that party I saw a chap I had seen around before who I always found amusing. He suggested that I go on with him to another party which he said would be great fun. 'There won't be many women,' he said, 'but plenty of men.' Of course I jumped at it, and off we went. Well. When we got there, there were about 150 men and not one other girl and all the men were homosexuals. They were calling each other 'honey' and 'darling' and kissing each other and dancing together. I sat there feeling acutely embarrassed. On one side of me sat a man who had designed costumes for the elephants at the circus that year (they were going as peacocks, I learnt) and on the other a man who was described to me as Osbert Sitwell's lady-in-waiting. I simply could not understand why I had been taken there. My rather disappointing evening ended with me taking a taxi home alone and being so flustered that I gave the taxi driver $5 thinking it was $1.

I was flustered the first time I went to stay with my cousins near Chicago, too. But for very different reasons. Almost the first thing I did when I arrived at their terribly grand house was to drop an open bottle of red nail varnish which went all over the pristine white carpet in the guest bathroom. It wasn't even a flat carpet, it was a tufty one so the nail polish went down between each strand of the thing. I scrubbed and I scrubbed but I could not get it off and in the end I had to come out and admit what I'd done. I needn't have worried; they were so nice about it, simply saying, 'We've just had it decorated. We'll just have it decorated again.' But happily, after that disastrous start to my stay, things improved. I seriously impressed them because I had a letter of introduction to the Annenbergs.

Walter Annenberg was a billionaire businessman and philanthropist who would later be appointed US ambassador to the Court of St James by President Nixon. He was also the man who introduced Margaret Thatcher to Ronald Reagan. Annenberg did more for Britain, through his quiet philanthropy, than any other ambassador, and almost more than any other American. A Midwesterner, from a Jewish family, he was used to the world of newspapers and magazines, not diplomacy; he had not been schooled in protocol. When he came to London as ambassador in the 1960s he was initially ill at ease and, alas, rather looked down on, even snubbed, by a great swathe of British society. Towards the end of his five years in Britain, he and his wife gave a lavish dance. A vast number of people found themselves ringing up the embassy to ask why they hadn't been invited. Had there been a mistake? 'No mistake.' That's all he said. It was his payback time. 'No mistake.' I love that.

But in 1950s America, I was on the Annenbergs' guest list, together with my cousins. I'd been introduced through friends of ours. My cousins were so excited you would have thought they were going to meet the Queen. When we got to the house, the door was opened by a butler. We were ushered down a corridor hung with Impressionist paintings into a beautiful drawing room, where tea was served by footmen. It was the most marvellous tea – little sandwiches, cakes, scones, everything. But I was the only one who ate it. My poor cousins were far too nervous to eat. I, on the other hand, ate like anything. But at least I didn't tap-dance on the table.

Tap-dancing was then my party trick – I was frightfully good at it in those days. I'd taught myself as a child, and had given tap-dancing lessons at my hateful schools in exchange for Mars Bars. In New York I'd become very friendly with a girl called Kline, whose father was a partner in the pharmaceutical company Smith Kline and French, which today is part of GlaxoSmithKline. Her parents lived in Philadelphia, and when their darling daughter moved to New York, they gave her a rail pass so she could easily go home to see them. Whenever I went to Philadelphia for the weekend (which was quite often, because for a time I had two boyfriends there. One was the American. The other had a very shocking mother who, on my arrival at her house, introduced herself and said, 'Why don't you go upstairs and lie down with my son.'), she lent me her pass. I was always so terrified that the guard would discover that I was English – and obviously not the person whose name was on the pass – that I used to sound rather like a bad Gary Cooper. The guard would say, 'You going far, miss?' And I'd say, 'Nope.' Then he'd say, 'Everything OK for you here, miss?' And I'd say, 'Yep.' 'Yep' and 'Nope' was all I'd say, all the way to Philadelphia.

It was in Philadelphia that I first tap-danced on a table, at a very jolly party. I'd never forgotten how to do it, and I suppose I was feeling rather happy at this party and I decided to show off my skills. I think I could still do it now, with a good partner and a little practice. I loved dancing. Another time I found myself dancing with Bob Storer, who'd made up the third in my skiing party with the American. He suddenly said, 'Let me bend you over my arm like a willow.' I was frightfully pleased and flattered and over I went, all six feet of me, at which point he groaned 'Timber!' I suppose he had seen me skiing so he was under no illusions about my elegance or delicacy. He became a great friend though.

When I wasn't in the Hamptons or dancing in Philadelphia, I spent many weekends with my dear friend Ronnie Furse. Ronnie – or Ronpon, as I called him – had a wonderful property on a place called Fishers Island, a small island off the tip of Long Island. You got there by ferry – although some very swanky people arrived by private plane. It was a few miles long and only a mile wide, practically uninhabited during the winter, but wonderful in the summer, with lovely cool breezes whereas New York was so often sweltering hot. There were always jolly nice people there and very good golf at the Country Club, but as with the Hamptons it was a very closed society. Ronnie was American, though you would never have known. He'd been educated at Eton and grew up at his family's enormous farm in Sussex. The Furses had lived in England for ages, but they had all kept their American citizenship: during the First World War somebody somehow upset them and as a result they never applied for British nationality. Ronnie had been a very good friend to David when he first moved to New York – it was Ronnie who had first scooped up David when he was penniless and ill, at the annual New York Old

Etonian dinner David had managed to drag himself to. He was the biggest picker-upper of people in trouble, simply the kindest man. He in turn became a very good friend to me. Everyone loved him.

Ronnie often took me to the theatre or the ballet in New York, too. I remember once that we went with his parents to see José Greco, the great flamenco dancer. Luckily his parents were quite deaf so did not hear my shrieks of '*Olé*' and '*Bravissimo*'. I got quite carried away and longed for Spain.

After I had been in New York only a few months, the American returned from Paris to Washington and I worked myself up into a complete *Ladies Home Journal* state of excitement about it. Our romance continued and I even met the American's mother at her house in Philadelphia. She had had it built as a complete copy of a French chateau and was enormously grand. I was quite frightened of her. I wish I could have known her now, when I am rather grand myself.

But despite his alarming mother, now the American was back on native soil we had some lovely trips away. One weekend I learnt to water ski at the Beverley Ski Club in Chesapeake Bay, which I felt was quite brave of me. I was doing it to show off to him of course. I had bought a bathing suit that I thought would be very suitable for the occasion, a white bathing suit, but I thought I

had better just test it out and so I leapt into the bath
with it on and came out of the bath all dripping wet.
And I said to the American, 'Can I wear it?' And he said,
'Absolutely not.' It was transparent. As it turned out I
hardly needed to worry about transparent bathing suits
because all was revealed anyway. The wind does some
pretty cruel things to your clothes when you go at that
speed and more than once I sank under the water on
purpose, just to stay decent.

Water skiing turned out to be tremendously exciting
– I loved the feeling of speed, and skiing through the
path of the setting sun on a warm winter's evening was
simply heaven – and frightfully tiring. Eventually you
fall off the skis through sheer exhaustion, which is a bore,
because you are then so done in you think you might
drown before you can get yourself somehow or other back
into the speedboat. I knew I was supposed to throw my
legs over the side but it didn't work: when you're tired
the sides of a boat seem very high. In the end they had
to pull me in and I was covered in bruises for days from
all the hauling.

Weekends with the American were heavenly, of course,
but so, too, was my social life. It was hectic to say the
least. At times it was also rather ridiculous. Through a
series of circumstances my parents knew a French actress
called Lilo. She had spent a weekend at their farm wearing

just a nylon shirt with nothing underneath and leopard-skin trousers. I was not at home at the time but had heard colourful accounts from my father and my brother Alastair, and a sinister silence from my mother. Lilo was about to open on Broadway, as the star of the new Cole Porter show, *Can-Can*. Despite the previous sinister silence, my mother wrote to me and asked me to be nice to her, and so I was. She was platinum blonde and small and curvy and I was all set to dislike her intensely but in fact she turned out to be awfully nice and rather lost. She had a six-foot azalea tree in her bedroom from Cole Porter, and the two boyfriends I took to meet her were quite enamoured, so I knew she would not be lonely for long.

Befriending French actresses was only a tiny part of the fun I had. I went canoeing on the Great Egg river in New Jersey (and capsized, causing tidal waves and shrieking laughter, and a sunk boat). I went sailing off Maine (and again capsized, but in the Atlantic, which was bloody cold). I went to the races in Saratoga Springs, where I got locked in the loo. (Even when I wasn't at the races, I was keeping a very close eye on what the horses were up to. In those days it was illegal to bet, except on the telephone or at the racecourse itself, so no one talked about racing or placed any bets. I did though. There was always an elevator boy who would be happy to take a bet on for you, but you'd better hope you were never caught.

It was a chancey life but it was a hell of a lot of fun and I made a few bob, too.) I stayed with friends from the war who had made their money through Caterpillar tractors: they were so rich they ate off solid gold plates but so down-to-earth they washed them up themselves. I watched Princeton play Harvard at American football on a beautiful day and afterwards went to the Ivy Club. I watched Maureen 'Little Mo' Connolly play tennis. I had dinner with Senator McCarthy, who was just as I had expected: loud and unlikeable. And I spent happy weekends in the country, whether in upstate New York, New Hampshire, Pennsylvania or on Long Island, at my friend John Lindsay's house. At the time I simply thought of John as damn good-looking and great fun. A few years later he was Mayor of New York. I stayed, too, at my friend Keith Eggleston's heavenly family home, Appleton Farm, in Ipswich, Massachusetts. The farm was full of animals – and not just sheep or cows. There seemed to be millions of animals wandering around the place, among them a large green parrot, six hunters, two donkeys, a greyhound, a cairn terrier, seven or eight other terriers, a poodle, some other birds and a pet raccoon. The raccoon was charming with a dear little foxy face, a very fat furry body and a lovely broad stripy tail. I fell for it in a big way and it quite liked me, which was a great compliment as it was very shy.

However, although I would go away for these marvellous weekends, I had no money at all apart from what I earned, which was not a lot. So every Monday morning, it was back to reality with a bump. Sometimes even the mid-week mornings were bumpy.

On one such memorable occasion we threw a party for another lifelong friend I had made while in New York, Michael Edwards, who was heading back to England. The party was suitably riotous and it finished with a drunken few heading out to La Rue's on East 58th Street. We closed La Rue's, then went on to El Morocco and closed that, too. I finally got to bed half an hour before I had to get up for work.

Come to think of it, I was so busy having a good time that I was lucky to have a job at all.

The job my brother had found for me was basically typing: I was secretary to the chief executive of the agency. But I did it so badly that he had to get rid of me. It was only because the chairman, who owned the company, was a friend of my brother's that they kept me on, as a kind of pet. It was a very odd place in some ways. Unusually for those days, one of the other people in the typing pool was a man – and a pretty low-class kind of a man, too. I remember I broke a typewriter running away from him. We all had to stay late and mend the damn thing otherwise we would have all got the sack.

After I had been in New York for about a year I moved into a flat in the same building as dear Ronnie Furse. My new flat was on the eighth floor of a big brownstone house at 137 East 73rd Street. It was huge, had a television and it was unbelievably cheap. I shared it with four girlfriends and I had a wonderful time, as you can imagine.

There was no question of interior decorating: it was pure practicality and comfort. But I did add a rather charming touch, I thought, when one day I discovered they were giving away the lilies in Rockefeller Plaza if you dug them up yourself. Everyone in the office thought I was mad as I scrabbled in the earth and then staggered home in the rain with the heavy pots full of mud, but the flat smelt divine for about a month.

Initially, Ronnie was appalled about me moving into his building. I think he rather expected me to be forever hanging over the bannisters in a dirty kimono, cigarette dangling, hair in curlers, watching the comings and goings on the stairs. He told me he made a point of never seeing the people who lived in the house. However, I didn't hang over the bannisters much and I did see a lot of Ronnie. He had a superb cook called Bessie who prepared wonderful dinner parties for him and who would come down and clean our flat when she had time. Or Ronnie would ring down and say, 'I have asparagus, come on up.' And up I would go. We played a lot of bridge, and gambled like mad.

Ronnie had lost an eye fighting at Monte Cassino during the Second World War. I remember being most put out when I went in his dressing room and found all his spare glass eyes sitting on top of the dressing table. I hadn't realized until then, although it did help to explain the way he drove – which was like a maniac.

Ronnie and I had some dreadful rows. He used to say the most maddening things to me – partly to irritate me, I felt – and I always rose like a fish. And I used to take a vicious pleasure in shocking him. But I grew terribly fond of him, and him of me. He was the most wonderful friend although I felt he was rather lonely, and I longed to find some nice girl for him.

Ronnie's still alive today and he rings me up regularly. Sadly, we have the most frustrating conversations because he's deaf as a post, so he can't hear anything I say.

I loved my life in New York, although I did hate being so broke. The only thing I missed about London was my flat: although it was now let out, I still thought of it as home. But I am not sure I could have ever been enticed back to London for good – despite my parents becoming increasingly crackly on the subject – if it hadn't been for Barker.

CHAPTER NINE

Barker

In May 1952, on one of my many weekends away, I met a man called Alan Barker. He was a master at Eton, and was in the States on a Harkness Commonwealth Fellowship to Yale University.

I'd been invited to stay by Tom Mendenhall. Tom had been a Rhodes Scholar at Balliol College, Oxford, and was now at Yale, as Master of Berkeley College. He had asked a group of us down for the weekend. I didn't know the Mendenhalls terribly well but somehow I was part of the party. Ronnie was there, and a girl called Kate Williams, who became a lifelong friend. I remember we played field hockey – which I had never played before in my life – so I spent most of the weekend with a huge black eye. I liked Alan immediately I met him. He struck me because he had a personality and he had intelligence, which was quite rare in my life. We just sort of gelled.

Alan – whom I almost always called Barker – had

served as a captain with the Royal Artillery during the war and been shot in the thigh by a sniper while sitting on top of a tank on D-Day plus ten. They didn't realize how badly he had been injured until he became delirious. If it had not been for penicillin he would not have survived, and as it was he went through his undergraduate days in Cambridge in a wheelchair and ever after had a scarred and wasted leg. He walked with a limp his entire life. He also had a great fear of injections: back in the 1940s, a penicillin injection was like a kick from a mule. Barker had been born in Edinburgh, had gone to school at Rossall in Lancashire and had studied history at Jesus College, Cambridge, where he had been a member of the Pitt Club.

Before he went back to England, we ran into one another a couple of times – mainly at Ronnie's place in New York – and, after he left Yale, we corresponded, but just as friends. We gossiped about mutual acquaintances (of whom we had many) and about our lives. I still had boyfriends (including a chap who was the ex-middleweight champion boxer of Virginia University) and of course they featured in my letters too.

Then, a year after the weekend we first met, I flew back to England for the Queen's Coronation. The next three weeks were thrilling, exhilarating, the most blissful I can ever remember.

London at the time of the Coronation was like nowhere

you've ever been. Everything was decorated, everything was beautiful. Even on the day itself, when we had the most dreadful weather, pouring with rain. I had a lovely seat just opposite Westminster Abbey – thanks to the kindness of a very very good, platonic friend called Peter Tunnard who was in the Scots Guards – from which I had a marvellous view of all the private carriages as they drew up, including the Speaker's carriage, which weighed sixteen tons and had no brakes. Think about it: a) getting the horses to pull it and b) stopping it. But they did.

I'd come home for the Coronation, but while I was in London, I also went to the Trooping of the Colour, and the Royal Tournament and up to Eton for the Fourth of June. I went to the Derby and to Ascot. In fact, I went to everything.

But in those three hectic, divine weeks, I also fell in love with Alan and I think he with me. I had been harbouring a secret fancy for him of course, ever since our weekend at the Mendenhalls' place, and had had a premonition that something like this might happen. I found him cosy, and clever, and strong-minded enough to boss me and simply delicious. A lot of courting went on on a rather upright sofa at his digs. And then, on the way to a dance on the evening before I was due to fly back to New York, Alan asked, would I marry him. Of course I said yes. I then spent the evening quietly furious with him because instead of dancing with me, and looking after me, he went off to talk with his friends. I later learnt never to go to a dance with Barker because it would always be awful for me, sitting on the sidelines when I was longing to dance. He never danced if he could help it. I used to think it was just because he loved talking so much but now I wonder whether it was partly because of his bad leg. Back on the night of my engagement I hadn't worked any of this out. I was engaged, but not being showered with the affection that I thought would come with it.

The next day, I flew back to the States, not knowing when I would see Barker again. Having been reluctant to leave my wonderful life in New York three weeks earlier, I felt rather miserable and confused as I returned.

I don't remember a great deal about our subsequent courtship. It was, by necessity, conducted entirely by letter. I would send heartfelt missives, declaring my love and demanding similar declarations in return, signing off with such things as 'I miss you terribly and love you equally'. We scribbled to each other about friends we had seen, and about who we were: the music we liked, whether we liked to talk at breakfast. A courtship by letter is actually rather hellish because firstly one always misinterprets and secondly so much depends on the mood of the moment and thirdly it is simply gruesome waiting for the next letter to arrive. Transatlantic calls were impossibly expensive and usually didn't go through anyway.

At some point after I was safely back in New York, Alan went to meet my father. How I wished I could be a fly on the wall. I imagined them both terrified, facing each other over a couple of pink gins. But whatever happened at this meeting, and a subsequent dinner with both my mother and my father, it didn't seem to put Alan off, and I received letters from both my parents claiming to think that Barker was wonderful.

The engagement was announced in the *New York Herald* and the *New York Times* on 22 October 1953, and in *The Times* on 2 November. I had the picture taken for the announcement at *the* New York society photographers, Bachrach – what a performance that was – but my mother hated it: I was in a white blouse and she wanted me looking more glamorous, in evening dress, so she could put me in *Country Life*.

After Barker proposed, I had to break the news to the American. 'Oh Jean,' he said. 'Why couldn't we go on as we always have?' And I realized what a good decision I had made, because that would have been my life, for the rest of my days.

I think one has two loves in one's life. The American was my first and Alan was my second, but Alan was quite different from the American. I had a wonderful time –

and lots of fun – with the American but I didn't terribly admire him, and while I had found him silent and fascinating in France, I found him slightly snobbish and spoilt in America. Alan I admired so much.

*

I was soon terribly busy planning the wedding and attending the dozens of lunches and showers and cocktail parties and dinner parties my friends in New York threw to celebrate my engagement and mourn my departure.

A friend who worked for the fashion magazine *Harpers Bazaar* introduced me to the best maker of wholesale wedding dresses in New York. I went to an enormous warehouse in the garment district and ploughed through about a million dresses and finally chose a glorious, very ornate broderie anglaise wedding dress with a high neck and tiny covered buttons all the way down the front that cost nothing compared to anything I'd have found in England. Once I'd chosen it I had to be measured for it and a great crowd of people gathered round while the man measured my bosom about thirty-three times. After that, every time I went back for fittings, which involved being re-measured and re-re-measured, a great big black man would lean against the clothes rail and say, 'How's my little English cousin today?' He was lovely. My friend

Sally lent me her family tiara which was absolutely beautiful. If I was pushed over the years I would borrow it for diplomatic receptions but it's now with Samantha Cameron, who is the stepdaughter of Sally and Bill's son William. I wouldn't want the responsibility of borrowing it these days.

One evening just before I was due to leave for London, I was at one of Ronnie's dinner parties with a lot of old Etonians. 'Go on,' said Ronnie. 'Put your wedding dress on, we'd love to see it.' So I went downstairs to my flat, put it on, and then wafted back up. Ronnie's telephone rang – but it was for me. So I took the phone and found it was our neighbours across the street. 'Hi,' they said. 'We love your dress.'

Finally, on 15 December 1953, I set sail from New York. As I passed the financial district, I stood on deck and watched as all my dear friends waved like mad and emptied their waste paper baskets out of their windows in the traditional New York tribute to departing loved ones. It was like snow and it was simply lovely.

The journey took seven days. The plan was that I was to diet like mad and get beautifully thin for the wedding, but there was a flat calm and I ate my way to England. I was much fatter when I arrived than when I had left, and my mother marched me off to Dr Goller, a well-known diet doctor on Harley Street. His was the magic name if you wanted to lose weight. God knows what was in the pills he gave me, probably worms, but they worked and the pounds fell off.

Losing weight was easy compared with my living arrangements, though. I had expected to join my parents in the tiny flat they now owned, in Eaton Mews North, at least until the wedding. But my moving in meant that the cook had to move out. I had slept there one night when she confronted my mother, saying, 'If you make me do this you'll have to get a new cook.' The cook was obviously more important to my mother than I was, so once again, at the age of thirty-one, I was homeless. Luckily, as usual, I had friends who took me in – Peter Tunnard and his sister. They lived just round the corner and it was so kind of them, which is more than my parents were, frankly.

I knew my father loved me dearly though. The night before I married I moved back into their flat and slept in his bedroom (my mother had twin beds in her room, but mostly he slept in the lovely big bed in his dressing room). I didn't get much sleep because I was so nervous about my wedding day. My father came into the room in the morning and he was obviously dying to say 'I really love you', but he couldn't do it. He went round and round the mulberry bush. And although I knew exactly what he was trying to do, I couldn't help him.

You can't say to someone, 'I know you love me.' They have to make the supreme effort. He didn't manage it. And he made up for it by being horribly bad-tempered all day.

*

The wedding ceremony itself took place at the Chapel of the Royal Hospital in Chelsea, which I still think is the most beautiful place to get married in the whole of London, on 18 March 1954. It was very unusual to be married there in those days – in fact, I think there had only been one other wedding there since 1815. It was certainly very difficult to arrange, but somehow I managed to do it. I don't know quite how. I only remember that I wrote to the governor telling him how much I loved the chapel and how beautiful I thought it was. I ended my letter, 'Please may I get married there?' Rather marvellously, he wrote back saying that although he received endless requests, he knew that most of them were full of silly stories to try to persuade him to agree, and he was so pleased that I'd simply told the truth he was going to say yes. The downside was that I would need a special licence from the solicitor general to get married there, which didn't please my father at all, because it cost £25. My mother was furious too because she had wanted me to be married in All Souls, Langham Place, where she and my father had been married.

My poor old dress had been going in and out, in and out, every time I lost or gained a pound. But the final diet had worked like a charm. As I walked down the aisle to the strains of Purcell's 'Trumpet Tune and Air', I heard someone say, 'What a waist.' Either that, or 'What a waste.' Alan and I both heard it, but we never ever knew how they were spelling it. Was it a comment on my hard work dieting, or was it someone with their eyes on Barker? Or perhaps on me?

My New York friend Patsy Shepherd was my brides-maid and Sue and Charles Graham's two boys, James and Malise, were pages. Barker's best man was his friend Giles St Aubyn, who was also a history master at Eton. Giles, who never married himself, did a very thoughtful thing for me that day. During the reception, I went upstairs to change into my going away outfit and as I came back down he happened to be in the lift with me and he said, 'Take your ring off.' Without thinking, I did so. Then he said, 'You did that without thinking, but you will be glad you did. So many women I know become fixated on the idea that they can't ever touch their wedding ring. If you take it off on the day itself and put it back on, you know you can.' It was so sweet of him.

Giles' presence was doubly important, somehow, because Barker hadn't invited his father to the wedding.

His parents were divorced and he didn't like his father at all. I only met him once: he rather overdid his attempts to be charming and as a result I didn't like him one little bit. Even so I thought it was most unfair not to invite him to the wedding. Barker's mother was a lovely woman and highly intelligent and she adored Barker. But we didn't see much of her after we were married because she went out to live in Rhodesia where Barker's twin brother Tom had settled. I rather think I frightened her.

There were around 500 guests and I got some divine wedding presents. My mother, being an interior decorator with a very beady eye for a bargain, knew the value of each and every one: she was furious about the vase that her friends the Trittons gave me (which I thought was simply charming): Elsie Tritton's first husband had been Sir Louis Baron, who had made a fortune from Black Cat cigarettes, and her second husband, Robert, was a great collector of beautiful things so she felt they should have done a lot better. But Ma couldn't complain about the gifts I received from two American fellows who were both great friends of mine. One of them gave me $100. The other one, Joe McCrindle, who had been my 'sponsor' in the US, said, 'I'm not going to be outdone by him,' and so he gave me $101. I spent most of it on clothes.

Afterwards, I threw my bouquet at my great friend

Diana Lyttelton, who was then assistant press secretary to the Queen, the first woman to hold such a post, and whose brother was the jazz musician Humphrey Lyttelton. She was madly in love with someone who didn't love her – that old old story – and as a result she was still not married. I was terribly fond of her and we were all very worried about her. The bouquet must have done the trick though because in 1957, when she was thirty-seven (which in those days was considered positively ancient to be a bride), she married Alexander Hood and they immediately had three sons, bang, bang, bang.

Barker and I spent our honeymoon on a driving tour through France and Spain, in Alan's soft-topped Ford. We set off from the Dower House at Knowlton, which was meaningful to both of us. For me, Knowlton was the scene of my childhood friendship with Robin Speed, who had been killed in the war. Barker was in fact great friends with Robin's aunt and uncle, Enid and Dudley de la Farge, who lived in the Dower House. Enid and Dudley were one of the reasons we had come to know each other so well, so it was very apt that we started out from there. The car broke down several times on the trip, including on the dock in England: we had to be pushed into the boat. But it didn't matter at all. In fact, it was the most riveting journey I'd ever been on because Barker, being a historian, always knew fascinating things to tell me and found interesting places to go. He had a story about everywhere we went, even places we were stuck in while we got the car fixed. On our return, we moved to Cambridge, and a new chapter began.

CHAPTER TEN

Cambridge and Eton

When I had first met Barker at Yale, he had been a master at Eton, but during our courtship, he had taken up a history fellowship at Queens' College, Cambridge. So it was in Cambridge that we began married life together. Our little house on Richmond Terrace cost us £800 — which was nothing, even then — and was tiny and sweet and perfect. It had a little sitting room, a dining room, a kitchen and a bathroom downstairs, and three bedrooms: one became our room, one Barker's dressing room and one the spare room.

Those were very carefree days. Alan had an enjoyable job as a don, and since he had been both a master at Eton and an undergraduate at Cambridge not many years earlier (his studies having been interrupted by the war), he knew simply everyone. Consequently, I had lots of young men around and I played tennis madly with them all at the public courts at the end of the road. I knew a lot of people myself too, from my time at Bletchley, because Bletchley had been full of dons from Oxford and Cambridge. I'd been so dreadfully naughty there though that if ever a don from Bletchley saw me on the street he would say, 'Oh no, not you!' and run off in the other direction.

To my delight we got a dog: a simply adorable long-haired dachshund whom we named Sherry-Netherland Barker, or Sherry for short. (The Sherry-Netherland is a big hotel in New York, near Central Park.) I did put Sherry in for a show once because she was so pretty but we sat on the floor of the Guildhall for hours and hours and then she bit the judge. I can't remember whether we got any certificates, but I rather suspect not.

One small fly in the ointment was that my early attempts at cooking were a bit hit and miss, and sometimes dropped as well. My first tossed salad was tossed straight in the dustbin because I made it with a cabbage and not a lettuce. But I practised, and I got better. I discovered I had a talent for making things taste good, and with time I learnt to make them look good as well. My early attempts at entertaining were similarly disastrous. The first thing I did was to invite the porter to tea, confusing the college porter with the college master. They are, of course, very different things. There were a lot of undergraduates around when I issued this invitation and they killed themselves laughing. I had no idea

I was doing anything peculiar. To his great credit, the porter still came to tea and a jolly nice time we had.

This easy, pleasant life lasted about a year. Barker and I had married in March 1954 and by March of the following year I was pregnant. Barker spent a lot of time in his rooms at Queens' College and I was alone in our little house, either feeling sick or craving porridge. And then, in July, a month before Adam was due to be born, we left our lovely little house in Cambridge – selling it for £1,500, which thrilled me – and moved into a horrid little house in Eton.

The funny thing is that I now can't quite remember why or how it happened. I have a feeling that Barker was disappointed when he realized he wasn't going to be made Professor of American History. And at the same time he was asked to become headmaster at some public school or other. He wrote to Robert Birley, his old headmaster at Eton, asking for his support – and I suppose a reference. But Birley wrote straight back and said, don't do that. Instead, he told Barker to come back to Eton. Birley would give him back his job and seniority, he should stay for three years to get some more experience and then go and be a headmaster. It was very good advice.

My father was far from happy with this change of direction. He had had a very unhappy time at Malvern College as a boy, and had developed a hatred of all school masters, on principle. 'They are all out to either make you or break you,' he used to say. But despite such objections, Barker took the job.

By the end of August, Adam was showing no inclination to be born, and I had to be induced. I went into the Princess Christian Nursing Home, Windsor, at 10 a.m. on 31 August 1955. At five o'clock that afternoon, in the middle of a game of Scrabble with Barker (who was – most unfairly – winning), labour finally started. The labour wasn't long, but it was difficult: Adam was rather insisting on being born sideways. Eventually they had to call a specialist. All I can remember is the big white chief bending over me and saying, 'We'll have one more try of turning him around and if not we are going to do a caesarean. Do you understand?' Yes, I did. They managed it, and at 11.30 at night, out he came: 8 lb 3 oz and a bit battered, because they had been trying like anything. I was a bit battered too.

Adam was the only baby in the nursing home when he was born, and then the next day a second baby arrived at the home, a girl called Eve. Can you believe it? Adam and Eve. They wanted to make a great fuss about it but I wouldn't let them.

Adam's chief characteristics, as noted in the baby book (soon abandoned) were a very large head, Alan's nose and my ears (which were immediately taped back, to make them flat). He went straight onto Cow & Gate full cream, which he loved, and was a terribly good baby with a great interest in life. After the standard two weeks in the nursing home I took him home, and in November he was christened at Eton. There aren't many people who have been christened in that soaring fifteenth-century chapel with its Flemish-style wall paintings and magnificent stained glass. Nor who have two sets of godparents (one from the US and one from Britain): Osla, Michael Edwards, Ronnie Furse, Giles St Aubyn, Nancy Bruce Storer (married to Bob Storer) and Enid de la Farge.

*

Our horrid new house was on Eton High Street, next to Gaines' shoe shop. It was a strange little place. There was a sort of downstairs, partitioned off from the shoe shop, to make a study on the ground floor, furnished by my ma, where the boys could come in to see Barker for what was called 'private business' – one of the many Eton rituals with which I was to become familiar. You had to go under the staircase to enter the kitchen, which happily was big, and a scullery which was also big. The staircase was very steep and at the top was a bathroom on the left, Adam's so-called day nursery straight ahead, and a kind of made-up room which was where Wilma, the Austrian au pair, slept. I did the cooking and she did the cleaning and took care of Adam and did everything else, and I paid her £3 a week. There was also a little sitting room, Adam's bedroom, our bedroom, and through our bedroom a little cubby hole with a bed for if we had guests. It was a very cobbled-together sort of house.

It wasn't easy in the summer because we didn't have a garden. Friends who did – other masters' wives – felt sorry for me and were very generous. One of them said I could come any time I liked, and I did. It was very awkward though because she had a dog that used to bite. I was always having to haul my poor Sherry into the air by the neck to protect her from this horrid dog. Eventually I lost my temper and really went for this woman. My father was there for some reason, and he was very shocked by my behaviour. He forced me to write to apologize, but I wrote a letter saying, 'This is my letter of apology, I have been asked to write it.' It was barely an apology at all.

As a new mother, I used to walk Adam in his pram up and down the High Street, up and down. There were about five antique shops there at the time, and I spent a lot of time in them. I became such good friends with the owners that they used to let me go into their back rooms and pick out whatever I liked. I learnt a lot from them. I had always loved colour and texture, and had a good eye for beautiful things. I had a good grounding in art from my time in Montrichard and Paris. Now I became knowledgeable about furniture, china and glass. And they were very generous to me, because I couldn't ever really afford anything at the right price. I've always been a great lover of bargains and I am still quite incapable of passing an antique shop without having a look.

Once I found a beautiful wooden lazy Susan that was priced at seventy-five shillings and the lovely man let me have it for almost nothing. It sat in the middle of the dining table and could be turned around so that people could reach the salt, the side dishes and so on. I gave it to my mother for her birthday and she was thrilled. It was so rare that I pleased her – usually she would just throw away the junk on which I had lavished my affection – but she loved that object and had it copied for all her clients. I got big plus marks there. In her eyes, I think it was the best thing I ever did. (On her death, I reclaimed it.)

The walking up and down with the pram didn't exactly help my back, which was already bad from playing all that tennis as a child, and had been made much worse by the pregnancy and birth. During Adam's early years I was constantly in agony and often in nursing homes. I tried all kinds of things over the years, and ended up in a steel corset. It was very hot in the summer, and very uncomfortable. Eventually my mother took me to a neurological surgeon who told me to throw away all that stuff and try to touch my toes twelve times a day. I did, and it worked. Extraordinary. But by that time I had spent my thirties encased as if in concrete from neck to waist.

Because of my back problems, and with David and his family always living abroad, my mother saw more of Adam than she did of her other grandchildren. Even so, I wouldn't go as far as to say that my mother was a better grandmother than she was a mother. Children bored her: interior decorating was what she loved. But she did adore Adam. When we were staying at their tiny mews flat in London, and they were entertaining friends for lunch upstairs, she would set up a kind of a barrier to keep a two-year-old Adam in my father's dressing room, which was opposite the dining room. Adam would peer over it and make faces and she just loved it. My father always had his back to Adam so he didn't know what was going on.

Eton was a funny old life. Fascinating, of course: very grand and very affected and not like other public schools at all. House masters were far from dim and not at all boring. They were grand, autocratic figures, and so were their wives. 'Darling,' said Grizel Hartley, one of the grandest wives, when I first arrived, 'if they won't eat anything else, they will always eat strawberries and cream.' Two other house masters, who were brothers, never spoke to each other due to some ancient feud. The story goes that one was walking up Eton High Street and the other was walking down, and the one walking up said, 'Spring in the air, Tommy old boy.' To which came the reply, 'You spring in the air yourself, Bill.'

There were endless special words – teachers were beaks, mid-morning break was chambers; special clothes – the famous nineteenth-century uniform of top hat and tails; special food – Eton mess, which is a popular pudding with everyone now, and Tap cutlets, which was an enormous piece of meat between two pieces of bread that has not entered the mainstream in quite the same way; and umpteen special traditions – like the boys giving portraits of themselves to the beaks when they left. There were special societies too. The most exclusive of these was Pop, whose members were Eton's prefects. The boys were all very keen to be invited to join and those who did wore special waistcoats, had special beating rights, and were themselves quite untouchable.

The school wasn't confined to a site like other public schools. Instead it was spread over the town. It didn't have dormitories like other schools either: the boys lived in houses, literally large private houses, and each of them had their own bedroom. There were real coal fires and it was the junior boys' job to refill the coal scuttles and generally slave, or fag, for the other boys. The most senior boys in each house had the right to beat anyone in their house who misbehaved. It was all quite feudal but it doesn't seem to have hurt anybody.

The boys had a particular kind of clever humour. One of my favourite examples of this concerned Betty Roe, the wife of a frightfully grand house master called Nicholas Roe. In each house there was a board on which notices could be written. And on this board, Betty Roe had written, 'Mrs Roe cannot conceive why the boys made such a lot of noise in the hall last night.' And all the boys did was re-punctuate it. 'Mrs Roe cannot conceive. Why? The boys made such a lot of noise in the hall last night.' That's a very Etonian joke. The little devils used to play a kind of cricket in chapel as well, awarding so many runs to visiting preachers or choirs, using a very precise set of rules. And everyone had nicknames. One beak's wife was very fat and was known as The Eclair Express. I don't think I had a nickname. And if I did, I never knew what it was.

Although Barker wasn't a house master, boys used to come to our house every evening for private business. This was basically a weekly meeting between the boys and their subject tutors. But it was up to Alan what he did with them; he didn't have to stick to drilling them in history. He could play it any way he wanted. He usually read them a book or played them some opera or talked to them about anything he liked. Sometimes the boys used to make their way into the kitchen (by then my cooking had greatly improved). Sometimes we would teach them bridge. I think it's terribly useful in life to be able to play bridge and tennis: it means you will always have friends and always get invited to places, if you are any good. Barker's favourite pupil was a very clever scholar called Douglas Hurd. Barker adored Douglas and I often heard them going hammer and tongs arguing some point or other at private business. Funnily enough, I found recently that Barker had kept some of Douglas' essays amongst his papers.

There was a strict hierarchy at Eton, and a terrific amount of gossip and snobbery. I was lucky because one house master's wife, Jane Brocklebank, knew my mother. In fact, my mother had been very kind to her after her father had gone to prison for some kind of fraud: in those days, if your father went to prison, you had a difficult life, but my mother had not cut off Jane Brocklebank, and had continued to invite her for dinner and so on. Jane, now married to a house master at Eton, paid me back in a big way. She was terribly kind to me and took me to Constance Spry cookery classes. Constance Spry was the Delia Smith of that time and founded the Cordon Bleu Cookery School. And Jane would then commission me to make things for her, so that I could make a little money. Once she asked for a dozen brioche. They are quite difficult to do and you've really got to learn how, and in those days I could do them. Other beaks' wives caught on and asked me to cook for them too: *babas au rhum* and so forth. I was less delighted about another family connection. One beak had been delivered into the world by my father's father when he had been surgeon general in India, and his wife had been to school with my mother. I could never walk down the High Street without her yelling at me, 'How's your mother?' I found it rather difficult, when I was just trying to quietly get on and make some friends of my own.

And then, joy of joys, we were invited by Grizel Hartley and her husband Hubert to dinner, which was like getting an entrée into heaven. Grizel was a great character and, as I've said, quite the grandest of all the beaks' wives. I confess that I didn't find her immediately loveable, but evidently she was very loveable – and even loving – to the boys and other masters. Hubert didn't speak a lot, because she did all the talking required. Later, Grizel published a collection of her letters from that time and I discovered that this joyful dinner featured in the book. She said, 'The new beak's wife has arrived. Her father is an upholsterer.' The idea! Well, my father would have just died. He was nothing of the sort. It was my mother, and she was an interior decorator. Nevertheless, it was true that we were socializing above our station really, with

Barker being only an assistant master. One friend, also married to a beak, used to infuriate me by standing outside my house with her daughter in her pram, just to see who was calling on me. I thought that was a bloody cheek.

Three years after we arrived, when Barker was still only thirty-five, and just as headmaster Birley had predicted, he was made headmaster at The Leys School in Cambridge. We were moving on again. Although I had been at Eton only a short time, it had been my brother David's school and Barker had taught there for a total of six years. For these reasons, and perhaps because it was where Adam was born, and perhaps, too, because Eton is such a very peculiar place, it would always remain very much a part of our lives.

CHAPTER ELEVEN

The Leys

Our arrival at The Leys in the summer of 1958 marked the beginning of the happiest and most settled time of my life. Alan was headmaster there for seventeen years. I brought up my son, put down roots and threw myself into life. I didn't think about it at the time, but I now realize that it is rather funny, given how much I had loathed boarding school as a girl, that I was so happy living in a school as an adult.

There were black moments, of course. On the day we arrived at The Leys, my poor Sherry was run over and killed in the school grounds. Can you imagine, the new headmaster arrives and his dog gets killed? I think Alan was even more upset than I was.

In 1962, my mother died. She had been crippled with diabetes and its complications for years, and managed to hang on just long enough to see her younger son Alastair married. Even in those dying days, though, it was my brother David she really loved. I remember being there with her in the nursing home towards the end, and David walked in – he'd been sent for – and her face lit up. It was rather touching.

After a difficult few years in which my father's finances were a constant source of anxiety to my brothers and me he remarried – much to my surprise and relief. A Scottish lady called Margaret, who lived in California, picked him up on a cruise. It had come to the point where we were pressing my father to give up his White's membership, so we were grateful that he had found someone to look after him. But then in 1970 I lost my father too. I had been to see him in London that day and he had been in bed. We had had a little conversation about his fading eyesight and so on. I had just made it back to Cambridge when I took a call to say that he had got out of bed to watch the six o'clock news and dropped dead. Lovely for him, just to go like that with no lingering illness and no pain. But awful for the rest of us. I am afraid I rather fell out with my stepmother after his death. I took her back to Cambridge with me that night, because I wanted to be kind: I didn't want her to be alone. The next day I had to go to a garden party I was opening: I didn't want to go, but I simply could not put them off at such late notice. I only left Margaret for an hour but she never forgave me. She said, 'You just dragged me down here

20. At the Stork Club, 1953.

21. The first photograph I took of Barker, at a house party
in Connecticut.

22. Barker and I leaving after our wedding, March 1954.

23. Barker holding Sherry and me holding Adam, aged two weeks, September 1955.

24. Take Your Pick – with Michael Miles and the prize wardrobe.

25. A summer stay at Cliveden in the early sixties.

26. With Adam and Barker at Cliveden, New Year 1962.

27. The Headmaster, his wife and the prefects of The Leys.

28. With Adam, Christmas 1970.

29. Barker outside his study in the garden at Luckboat House, Sandwich.

30. With Barker and Michael Edwards at their joint fiftieth birthday party.

31. Vote for Barker.

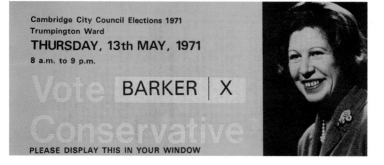

Cambridge City Council Elections 1971
Trumpington Ward
THURSDAY, 13th MAY, 1971
8 a.m. to 9 p.m.

Vote **BARKER** | **X**

Conservative

PLEASE DISPLAY THIS IN YOUR WINDOW

32. The notorious sponsored swim.

33. Giving the RAF the Freedom of the City of Cambridge.

34. My introduction as a member of the House of Lords, with my supporters, Rab Butler and Peter Thorneycroft.

35. At Buckingham Palace, with Adam, his wife Elizabeth and their daughter Virginia, after receiving the DCVO.

36. At my ninetieth birthday party, with my grandchildren
Virginia and Christopher.

37. At Newmarket, feeding Polo mints to Frankel on
my ninety-first birthday.

and then you leave me all alone. You are just making use of me.' We had a terrible row and I am afraid I never saw her again.

My greatest sadness over these years – and really the greatest sadness of my life – was that although I tried and tried like mad, I never got pregnant again. I would have loved another child, for myself and for Adam: I don't really approve of only children. Adam had been conceived so quickly and effortlessly that it was difficult to understand, but I suppose I was quite old by that time – I was nearly thirty-three when I had Adam – and perhaps the induction and all the turning of the baby had caused some damage. Every month I hoped. Any slight twinge of pain and I immediately thought I was, and then I wasn't. The doctors said there was nothing wrong, but it just didn't happen. There was no IVF in those days: if you couldn't, you couldn't.

But those were the only clouds in a clear blue sky. I had a happy son and a fulfilled husband, a lovely house not too far from London, wonderful friends whom I could visit, and whom I could entertain and have to stay, and a great deal of liberty. I loved all my neighbours, and most of the masters. I don't think anybody could have had a better time, I really don't. It was a heavenly life.

Adam grew into a wonderfully gutsy and independent little boy. If he wanted to do something, he did it – and

I admired that greatly. We had a dreadful winter in the early sixties, when Adam could only have been six or seven. I'll always remember it. Most of the boys at the school were out playing ice hockey on the fields where they would usually have played rugger, and the sunken lawn in front of the chapel had become a skating rink. Adam didn't have any skates – I wouldn't have bought them for him at that age, when he was growing like mad – but he went off and found some white ladies' skating boots from somewhere (begged, borrowed or I don't know what) and strapped himself in and off he went. Stepping out, turning round, falling down, all on his inside ankles – it was frightfully brave. He was the same with horses. A friend of mine who was a cavalry colonel taught him: Adam simply got up on the horse and off he went.

Another time, we went to see the building works going on at a friend's farmhouse. When we got there the house was locked and my friend said, don't worry, we can pop Adam through the dining-room window and he can go round and open the door for us. Adam was about eight at the time. So we popped him through, but what neither of us realized was that there was no floor in the dining room. Adam bravely jumped down fifteen feet, brushed himself off and opened the door for us.

Adam's determination meant that when he announced at the age of eleven, while lying in the bath, that he would go anywhere else but he wouldn't go to Eton, Barker and I quickly agreed not to try to persuade him. Adam felt strongly that at Eton he would always have been 'Barker's son'. He wanted to make his own way and be his own person. I greatly admired such independence of spirit, though it was a costly decision: Adam couldn't have known and indeed didn't know until years later, but as the son of a former beak Eton would have taken him for £100 a year. Instead, we sent him to King's School Canterbury and he had the most wonderful time there, playing lots of tennis and other games, and doing all kinds of naughty things. When he was about sixteen he got into particular trouble for cycling from Canterbury to our house in Sandwich with a couple of friends and drinking everything in our drinks cabinet.

I used to long to see him once he was at school, but he had reached that age where he didn't want me anywhere near him. I remember hiding in the bushes once all the way around a golf course so that I could watch him playing in a competition, with him shouting at me to go away. Another time he had a walk-on part in the school play in the wonderful ruined gardens around the Cathedral and he was determined not to recognize me. I don't know whether he was pleased that I was there, but he certainly didn't appear to be.

I think overall I was a good mother to him. I do feel

terribly guilty about one incident though. We were in
Italy, staying with my brother David. Having travelled
the world for J. Walter Thomson, he and Amy and their
three children had settled in Milan, where David eventually rose to become the firm's European director. We
often went to stay with them at their holiday house on
Lake Como, for blissful weeks of sunshine and wine and
evenings under the stars. It was at Lake Como that I found
the best hat I have ever known. Think of an upside-down
bucket made out of straw, with two eye-shaped holes cut
into it halfway down covered with coloured transparent
plastic. You could wear the hat all the way over your face
in the fiercest sun and still see out. Heaven! I had it for
years but then lost it in a house move and I've never been
able to find a replacement. I don't know why no one has
ever copied it.

On this particular holiday, Adam must have been six
or seven. We had decided to drive back to England slowly,
taking in visits to friends in lovely spots. One night we
stayed at a simply charming chalet up in the Swiss mountains and the following day we drove on in Alan's awful
ancient car to visit my old friend Solange Le Franc – now
Solange Fournier – at her beautiful chateau. On the way
there, Adam was sick all the time – by which I mean,
throwing up – and white as a sheet, and complaining of
stomach ache. I am afraid I wasn't very sympathetic. At

one road-side stop after another I told him he was simply car sick, or it was a stitch, and to get back in the car and take deep breaths.

However, when we arrived at the chateau I felt his forehead and realized it was hot. I decided that he really might be ill, so Solange was very kind and drove us back the twenty miles to see a doctor in Tours (who confirmed his temperature continental-style, with the thermometer up the bottom). The doctor told us to get back in the car, drive like hell for England and get him operated on the moment we arrived. So we drove off from Tours to Paris, where we stayed overnight with a cousin who lived there, with Adam still white and sick and now screaming in agony. The following day we made it back to England and Adam's appendix was removed.

Adam held that against me for many years. I am not sure what exactly he was so cross about: whether it was the fact that I told him he was only car sick, or the overnight stay in Paris instead of driving through the night or the fact that I never disclosed to him how ill he really was. He just used to love to tell me, 'I nearly died because of you.' I thought I had done my best. You don't always know, as a mother, what to do for the best in these situations.

While Adam was growing up, Barker was busily being a bloody good headmaster of The Leys. He was the first non-Methodist headmaster at the school since its foundation by the Methodists for the sons of lay members in 1875, which was a testament to how impressive he was.

When we arrived in 1958, The Leys was a very nice but rather boring school. Barker upped its game and put it on the map.

J. Arthur Rank, the film producer and former industrialist, was a devout Methodist, and a notable old boy. Rank had quarrelled badly with the previous headmaster. Alan set about wooing him back and as part of his campaign we threw a grand dinner party for him. We gathered in the drawing room before dinner and Rank said, 'The last time I was in this drawing room I was beaten by the headmaster.' It wasn't a tremendous start. But he went on to tell the story and it was rather funny. The headmaster had said to Rank and eleven other new boys, 'Tomorrow is your first whole holiday. If you do something with your whole holiday so be it, but you are not to go – and when I say not, I mean not – you are not to go racing at Newmarket.' Of course, to a boy they had all gone to Newmarket. On the way back, Rank's bicycle chain had broken so instead of getting back with all the others he had been very very late and had been given a sound beating. At this point, Barker told Rank he didn't believe in beating and no boy was beaten at his school, by masters or by other boys. Whether that was what did it I don't know, but he went on to give the school rather a lot of money.

Barker also persuaded the Duchess of Kent, Edward Heath and the prime minister of Singapore to come to The Leys. And he got the Queen Mother to visit not once but twice – once in 1961 to open West House, a new extension to the school that had gone up thanks to Alan's efforts, and again in 1973. The first time, Adam was five years old and he presented the Queen Mother with a beautiful bouquet of flowers. After she had had tea with the prefects and inspected the Officer Training Corps and so on, off she went, but she left her bouquet behind. When I realized what had happened, I very carefully removed each flower from the bouquet and gave one to every prefect who had had tea with her, as a memento. Just when I was back from handing out the last one, the telephone went and it was the lady-in-waiting. The Queen Mother was terribly upset that she had forgotten her flowers. Could I please send them up to London? Well, no way was I going to be able to do that at this stage, so it ended up with me ordering another great bouquet and taking it up in the train myself, to the servants' entrance to Clarence House.

The Conservatives' 1970 general election campaign kicked off at The Leys, too. Edward Heath was visiting us on the day that the Labour government resigned –

Barker had invited him and I was by then the chair of the local Conservative party – so he had to launch his campaign from our playing fields. I remember walking round and round the cricket pitches with him that day, absolutely desperate because he wasn't the greatest talker at the best of times. But he did give a jolly good dinner! Not long afterwards, perhaps as a thank you, he invited us to Number 10. I hate going to dinners where they've messed up some fish thing to start with and then messed up something else. Ted Heath's menu was perfection: blinis to start with, with caviar, followed by roast grouse, followed by fresh raspberries and cream. None of it was heavy, all of it was tasty. It was the most perfect menu ever.

In 1971 Barker offered the school's hospitality to Reginald Maudling, the then Home Secretary, who was in town to address the Cambridge University Conservative Association. At the time, there was huge controversy about Maudling's decision to expel a Cambridge student as an 'undesirable alien'. Rudi Dutschke, a socialist leader of the German student movement, had sought asylum in the United Kingdom following an assassination attempt in Germany, and was studying at Cambridge University, but was due to be deported the week of Maudling's talk. Fearing violent protests – this was only a couple of years after the events of 1968 – no one else would give the Home Secretary a billet. The visit went off with a huge police presence but without trouble. Barker insisted that it was about the right of our politicians to free speech.

As well as distinguished visitors we also welcomed some distinguished pupils. Bahrain and Tonga sent us their royalty to be educated. Every Tuesday a pale blue Rolls-Royce would arrive to collect the Prince of Bahrain's laundry and take it back to the Dorchester to be washed. It would have been perfectly well done at the school. The Prince always played rugger in tennis shoes and I later found out he had been ordered to. I don't think the poor boy terribly enjoyed life at an English public school. The King of Tonga used to visit quite regularly to see his son the Crown Prince, but always without warning, and I remember those visits as all being slightly panicky. Every time, I seemed to be sunbathing in my bathing suit in the private bit of the garden when Adam would rush in and say, 'The King is coming, Mum,' and I'd have to go dashing in to put some clothes on and arrange the chairs. There was only one chair he could sit on because he must have weighed twenty-five stone.

Alan didn't just go after the glamour pupils though. He was much more progressive than many headmasters were at the time about who he would let in. I remember there was one boy who suffered from terribly epilepsy. This boy bent pipes and did all kinds of things when he was having fits. Alan let him in, and the boys learnt to deal with him. Then, when a chap in the market place in Cambridge had a fit and lay writhing on the floor, everyone but The Leys' boys ran away. They, however, knew exactly what to do and stopped him from swallowing his tongue and so on.

*

My two boys, Alan and Adam, were happy, and so was I. One of my great happinesses was our wonderful new house. We moved, in 1958, from a poky little house next to a shoe shop to a handsome Victorian house of grey brick with private gardens, extensive grounds and plenty of room for entertaining.

To my great joy, we also bought a house in Sandwich, close to the beloved Rowling of my childhood, which became our home during most of the school holidays. Sandwich was a very odd but rather lovely affair in those days: I felt it was rather rundown high society without admitting it, full of old ladies hanging in there who had once been part of the Prince of Wales' circle. Indeed, the Prince of Wales used to love to play golf down at Sandwich, which is why the course there is called Royal St George's. These elderly ladies had retired to various cottages and made them lovely, and now spent their time playing bridge and golf. There was also a wonderful fur dealer and his wife called Provatorov. They had bought a very simple fisherman's cottage and done it up in the Russian style, panelling the tiny drawing room in white and gold for all they were worth. The Provatorovs invited the fisherman and his wife back to have a look at the old place. It was absolutely unrecognizable, as you can imagine, but the old fisherman opened the door to the drawing room, turned to his wife, and said, 'Look, Mother, it hasn't changed a bit.'

Our house was on King Street and we called it Luckboat House because the street had originally been called Luckboat Street, and otherwise, we were told, the name was going to be lost for ever. Neither of us had any money, but a rich friend of Barker's lent us the £900 we needed. It took us ten years to pay him back. I adored that house: my heart is in Sandwich, to this day.

But even more than the houses, I loved being the headmaster's wife. Absolutely loved it. When I first arrived I was rather intimidated because my predecessor had been American and terribly good at it. She had done everything right, and I felt I was bound to do everything wrong. Another of my predecessors, Mrs Bisseker, had a plaque dedicated to her in the chapel: 'To Mrs Bisseker, who lived for and was loved by the boys.' I used to stare and stare at that plaque. Boy, did I hate Mrs Bisseker!

I don't suppose any school ever had a more eccentric headmaster's wife, who smoked and drank and did everything naughty. But I gradually found my own way. The great thing was to be a sort-of mother figure for the boys, but not to interfere, ever. Unless asked. And not to have favourites.

I felt I was rather good at the mother figure bit.

Sometimes when it rained I played carpet bowls along the long corridors, with a beautiful and very rare and sought-after eighteenth-century set of wooden painted balls I had found in an antique shop. When it was time for the school photo, with the boys all arranged in rows and feeling very bored, I danced around in my bathing suit behind the photographer to make them smile for the camera.

I also cooked and cooked and cooked for them, and it was such a pleasure. (On the odd occasion when it was just the three of us, Barker would swoop in, put together anything he could lay his hands on in a sort of stew and call it 'Daddy's gumbo'. Adam and I had to suffer and eat it.) Every Sunday I made lunch for the visiting preacher, any governors who happened to want lunch, members of staff and a handful of boys. I saw these occasions as an opportunity to teach the boys decent manners. Because not all of them did have decent manners. Decent manners, to me, means that if you get an invitation, as a schoolboy, to lunch on Sunday, then you reply. If a boy didn't reply and then tried to turn up, I used to say, 'Sorry, I haven't heard from you, I am not expecting you. Goodbye.' It taught them. I taught them to say thank you, too, and received some killingly funny thank you letters from them.

I also undertook to teach the boys some culture. I took every new boy on one of Mrs Barker's culture tours. It was nothing to do with the school in a way. I simply felt that if they were living in Cambridge they had to be shown the wonderful things – the feast of possibilities – that the city had to offer. So I took them to the Scott Polar Research Institute to see Scott's letters, where I always cried: I couldn't help it. I took them to the Fitzwilliam Museum with its remarkable collections of objects, manuscripts and artworks, where the curators would open up cases especially for us. I took them to the Archaeology Museum, the wonderful Pepys Library at Magdelene College, the extraordinarily beautiful King's College Chapel – completed by Henry VIII just before he got busy destroying monasteries – and around all the great Cambridge colleges. Well, the thought that they should spend all those years in Cambridge and never see these things made me want to die. I thought that at least if they were taken once, then if they were interested they could go back again by themselves. The thank you letters were again wonderful, saying things like, 'Thank you for taking me to the Fitzwilliam Museum. I enjoyed trying on the Japanese armour but I didn't much care for the crockery section.' The crockery section being every kind of wonderful porcelain you can think of.

I was also almost always good at not interfering. I knew which boys smoked and drank and I never split on them. I only knew what one stupid boy was up to because I was walking up a nearby street and he was sitting in the window of a house, doing both. You couldn't miss it. When he left the school, he left fifty Woodbines on the hall table, with a note: 'With love to Mrs Barker.' I thought that was just lovely.

Occasionally, though, I couldn't resist interfering just a little bit. When Alan first arrived, he did, as I've said, ban any sort of corporal punishment. Instead, he made naughty boys cut his lawn (with a lawnmower, not with scissors or anything awful like that). I have to admit I used to feel sorry for them and rush out with chocolate biscuits.

My other great interference was over rowing. Alan was dead against it because rowing is such an expensive sport, but I was very pro. I thought it was ridiculous to have a school on the Cam and not row. So I wrote to Eton and said, 'Please could I have your cast-off boats.' A cast-off boat from Eton was as good as a new boat as far as we were concerned. I became the president of The Leys' rowing club and I was delighted to launch two boats for them.

Sometimes, too, I would be invited to interfere, and then it was all right, of course. Once, I think it was in the late sixties, Alan had a great problem with boys' hair. I was upstairs in my little private sitting room one Saturday, while Alan was having his usual time with the prefects in the drawing room, and Alan yelled up to me: 'I've got the prefects in the drawing room and I've tried to persuade them to have their hair cut and they don't want to know, so it's over to you.' Down I came, and I asked him, 'Are you sure?' Meaning, are you sure you want me involved? He said he was. So in I went and there they all were, sitting around in a rather casual way with their ghastly hair all over the place: come to think of it I don't think they even stood up for me. I said, 'In my day, hair like yours was known as buggers' grips.' And I walked out again. It was sort-of true, but it is not exactly what you would expect from the headmaster's wife in a Methodist school. It worked though. The next morning, in chapel, I looked over and saw that every single one of them had had his hair cut. Not a word was ever said about it again.

Only once did my behaviour really infuriate Barker. It was three weeks before the end of our last term. For seventeen years we had been at The Leys, and for seventeen years, on every Speech Day, it had been my job – my only job – to walk around the edge of the indoor swimming pool, terrified I would fall in, holding the various cups to be presented to the winners of the swimming gala. In this seventeenth year, when I had paraded around the pool for the final time, with the final cup, I jumped in, at the deep end, fully clothed, in my best Speech Day dress. The masters were astonished, the boys beside themselves with delight. Of course, almost the entire school followed me in, to 'save' me. Barker wouldn't speak to me for three weeks afterwards. I'm not surprised. It was so naughty. But so funny. I had suffered all those years and I just wanted a little bit of fun.

A master subsequently wrote and illustrated the most wonderful poem for me about the whole incident. It was a pastiche of Thomas Gray's 'Ode on the Death of a Favourite Cat, Drowned in a Tub of Goldfishes' and concluded:

> *But now, in petticoats maroon'd*
> *With hair bedraggled, skirts balloon'd*
> *She bobbed about serene;*
> *One little step into the deep,*
> *But this was mankind's greatest leap,*
> *O chlorinated Jean!*

I thought it was just wonderful and still have it, framed, in my kitchen.

*

I was blessed, through this period, as throughout my life, with some wonderful friends, old and new, who showed me great kindness and with whom I had enormous fun.

My old friend Al Friendly and his wife Jean became great pals (and epic bridge partners). I was quite brave because I simply rang him up when he was over in the UK as the *Washington Post*'s correspondent and said, 'Do you remember me from your transport at Bletchley? Come on down for the weekend.' So they came. It was only many years later that Jean confessed to me that when they had been invited that first time, she had been terribly reluctant to come. She had said to Al, 'Headmaster's wife. Provincial public school. Third class evening dress.' But apparently I had given the dinner party to end all dinner parties, with all the nobs there – including former Chancellor of the Exchequer Peter Thorneycroft, Master of Corpus Christi and former Permanent Secretary of the Treasury Frank Lee, and Home Secretary Reginald Maudling and their wives – and she had to admit that she had the most wonderful time.

Michael Edwards, whom Alan had known since Cambridge and I had known since my time in New York, and who now ran US Lines, a firm of passenger liners, remained a dear friend to both of us. He never married, though that wasn't because there weren't offers: I knew at least two women who desperately wanted to marry him.

Michael lived in Albany, the Palladian-fronted building next to the Royal Academy and opposite Fortnum & Mason. Originally built in the eighteenth century, it had been converted in the early nineteenth into 'chambers for bachelors' and living there was rather like living in a Cambridge college. Gladstone had had a set there, as had Lord Byron and Edward Heath. Michael and I used to take tours every August, around the snobbiest stately homes we could find. He was a wonderful companion, though I used to infuriate him by going to bed early, almost immediately after we'd had dinner.

Michael became such a good friend that when it came to their fiftieth birthdays, in 1973, I threw a shared party for Barker and Michael. The party took over the whole of the school and lasted an entire weekend during one half-term holiday. There was dinner in the upper dining hall on the Saturday evening, with speeches of course, and then dancing or bridge followed by kedgeree in the cricket pavilion. The dinner menu was themed with jokes on our names and places that were dear to us. On Sunday morning there was breakfast in the lower dining hall and optional excursions – cultural or sporting – followed by a buffet lunch at the headmaster's house. The funniest thing was the sleeping arrangements. We put up all the guests – probably about 150 people – in the boys' rooms. Alan was spotted going around the entire school putting soft

loo paper in all the loos instead of the horrid Izal the boys
had to endure. The men didn't mind stripping off in the
communal bathrooms, but the women simply hated it
and almost refused to do it. The Belgian ambassador, an
old friend, spotted the notice on the back of the door of
the room he was sleeping in which read, 'The following
have slept in this room,' followed by a list of all the
boys who had lived there. He added his name, which
the boys of course loved when they discovered it.

I confess that I did mind slightly that I put on this
terrific party for Barker and Michael and hadn't had a
party myself when I'd turned fifty the year before, but I
suppose they felt that the party was partly for me as well.
And it was a hell of a party.

Michael died of a heart attack in 2002. He was found
dead on the tube at Cockfosters. The extraordinary thing
is, when I heard, I immediately thought of a terribly dirty
joke. I had rung him up not so long previously to tell
him it: a man on the tube turns to the man next to him
and asks, 'Is this Cockfosters?' 'No,' replies the second
man with a happy smile. 'It's mine.' It was awful to think
of that now, except that he would have found it so funny
too.

Michael's memorial service was held in St John's, Smith
Square, the magnificent baroque church and concert hall
in Westminster. It was packed out, because Michael had

been so well loved. A concert pianist played and then I was asked to speak. It was a hell of a thing to have to stand up there in front of hundreds of people. What I said was probably rubbish, frankly, but I finished up by saying, 'When I think of Michael, I think of sunshine, I think of wine, I think of honey, I think of dogs. I think of Provence and I think of the Île St Louis. I think of fun and laughter and music.' Everyone was thrilled because I had hit the spot. They had all been thinking of exactly the same things. I'm so pleased that Michael died before he could become an invalid. He would have hated all of that.

Another wonderful friend was Elizabeth Samuel, who was a bit older than me and rather adopted me because I played bridge. Every year, Elizabeth used to invite me to stay at her house for Ascot. Alan never went racing so it was just me.

The first year I made a terrible fool of myself. Jackie d'Avigdor-Goldsmid, another old friend who used to go to Ascot every year, said I could go to the Jockey Club rooms for lunch and so I did. I sat down at a wonderful table with a view of the finishing line, and ordered lobster, new potatoes and salad. The waiter said, 'of course' and off he went. Then he came back and asked me for my number. Of course I couldn't give one, because I wasn't a club member. I had to get up in disgrace and leave. I walked for miles trying to find something to eat and eventually had a hot dog from a stand.

Another year I broke the rules again. I was in the Jockey Club stand, where you must not make a sound, and I got so excited I totally forgot where I was and I shouted for my horse. 'Come on Ile de Bourbon, come on Ile de Bourbon.' The woman in front of me turned round and I nearly died, but she just said, 'Thank you,' and then she, too, started shouting, 'Come on Ile de Bourbon' as he came round the bend. By the end I had the whole place shouting and yelling and Ile de Bourbon won. It was just lovely.

Every year I thought I'd never be asked back but every year I was. All the other guests were gloriously beautiful, with the most wonderful clothes, and there I was. I didn't even try to keep up with them on beauty, but concentrated on having the jolliest time. Elizabeth herself was rather highly strung, and she hated the races so she didn't even go, but one of her other guests, David Montagu, would always drive me, and we would sing our way there and sing our way back. We knew all the words of all the old songs from the 1930s: all the American numbers, anything by Noel Coward. Four days of great glamour and great fun. I had a ball. I miss it so.

David Montagu (later Lord Swaythling) not only loved horse racing, but also bridge, art and smoking and we became firm friends. He was a director of his family's bank, Samuel Montagu & Co, from a young age, and its chairman from 1970. He and a group of his fellow bankers from all over the world used to meet up once a year – and these occasions of course had to be splendid beyond compare – with each bank taking its turn to host. One year, it was Britain's turn and the chairman of Nat West announced that they would host, in Bournemouth. 'Bournemouth my foot,' said David. 'We'll have it in Newmarket and Cambridge.' The next thing he did was to ring me up. 'And you, Jean,' he said, when he had finished telling me this story, 'will be responsible for all our needs in Cambridge.' That was quite a tall order but I wanted to please David so I rang around like anything. First I rang Corpus Christi, who have the best manuscripts in the world, which are paraded at the enthronement of the Archbishop of Canterbury and kept under lock and key in a darkened cell at all other times. I told them I had a lot of international bankers coming, and could we possibly come and see the manuscripts. The answer came back no. They were so bloody snooty. 'Oh,' I said, enraged, 'David Rockefeller will be disappointed,' and put the phone down. Half an hour later the telephone rang. 'We've had a little think and we would be delighted to open up our vault for David Rockefeller and your other bankers.' And I had the joy of saying, 'Too late, I've already changed the plan and we're going somewhere else.' I was so pleased with myself.

What I had sorted out in the meantime was even better; I had persuaded the Fitzwilliam Museum to let us have dinner there. There had only ever been one other dinner given there, and that had been in Queen Victoria's time.

When the great day came, I was put next to David's most important guest, who was a Japanese banker. I am afraid I cannot remember his name. We were served a sherry at the beginning of the meal, and I immediately took a sip of mine. Very little reached my lips and a lot went down my arm. You can imagine, I was mortified. I tried again and the same thing happened. By this time I had twigged what was going on so I turned to my Japanese neighbour and said, 'Would you like a sip of my sherry?' Of course, having perfect Japanese manners, he said yes. Moments later, he had sherry down his arm too. The cut glass had been cut too deeply in one tiny place, and had sprung a leak so that every time you tipped it you got soaked but never got anything in your mouth. We both found it very funny, and then I made a great fuss, which I felt I had to do, and the glass was removed. A few moments later, the very important Japanese banker said, 'You know, I would rather like that glass.' So out to the kitchen I flew, where they had hundreds of glasses all of which looked exactly the same. I hadn't a hope of finding it.

There was a happy ending though. On the final night of their visit, the Lord Mayor of London gave a dinner for the visitors. At the end of the speeches, the Lord Mayor asked the Japanese banker to come to the stage because he had something for him. And when he unwrapped the parcel, it was a beautiful glass, with one cut that went slightly too deep. He was thrilled – and wrote to me afterwards in rather Japanese English to tell me what fun he was having, playing his trick on all his colleagues.

The Cambridge end of the trip had been a lot of work for me, but I was happy to be able to do something for David in return for all the kindness he showed me over the years.

Barker and I also became close to the Adeanes, local landowners who were related in some way to my old friend Diana Lyttelton (now Hood). Lady Adeane was a quite wonderful woman who had little family but had sat for Augustus John at the age of about eighteen. The portrait shows her sitting on a bar stool, displaying a lot of leg, and it is just terrific. She was really quite mad and not always the easiest person but somehow we clicked. She had us for scrambled eggs and champagne every Sunday evening, and took me on wonderful tours of the Middle East in 1968. Coming through customs with her was quite an experience. They would ask, 'Have you anything to declare?' And this small rather odd-looking woman dressed in jeans would say, 'Yes: a diamond and emerald necklace, diamond and emerald earrings, and probably a bracelet as well. And then there's the ruby one. And the sapphire one. And then there's the plain diamond one.' And they would laugh, thinking nobody who looked like her could have that kind of thing, and say, 'Oh go on, you silly woman.' I would be standing there with my mouth hanging open. But she wasn't putting on an act, she was merely telling them the truth.

I remained great friends with both Sally and Bill Astor after they divorced. Alan and I spent many happy weekends at Cliveden in the late fifties and early sixties, with Bill and his second wife Philippa, and then his third and final wife Bronwen. We met some rather interesting people there, too.

Once in the late fifties Bill sat me next to the great English artist Stanley Spencer. He is now best known for his paintings of gospel scenes set in the English countryside, and his rather rude pictures, but I always preferred his landscapes, which were absolutely divine. He didn't give a damn about them, though, referring to them as his potboilers because they were the paintings he dashed off when he needed a bit of money. That dinner at Cliveden was terribly grand, as they generally were, with everyone in evening dress. Except Stanley, who was wearing grey flannel trousers and a jacket over his pyjamas. We never stopped arguing – talking of God, talking of sex, anything you liked. Everyone else there was rather stiff and there was me with my hilarious and eccentric and probably slightly unbalanced neighbour in his pyjamas.

It was at Cliveden, too, that I met Stephen Ward. Ward was an osteopath but I thought of him mainly as a masseur, and a rather good amateur draftsman. There was an artists' studio at Cliveden and Bill himself wasn't bad, but Stephen was really rather good. He never drew me but a lot of it went on. At the time, of course, none of us really had any idea what he was up to with Christine Keeler and Mandy Rice-Davies, but eventually it all came out and the poor man killed himself. I don't recall ever seeing Christine Keeler there but I do remember another girl, at lunch. There was a very stately butler, whom Lady Astor adored and who had been with the family for ever. This girl looked at Todd and said, 'I would like some more fucking potatoes, please.' Of course, in true Jeeves style, he went back and got them without blinking. Bill told me afterwards that it had cost him a lot of money to get rid of her. The idea that they have made a musical of Stephen Ward's life horrifies me; I think it is in the worst possible taste.

Another time when we were staying, the Queen came

to tea, although she'd really come to look at Bill's stud. They kept the less presentable young ladies out of the way on that occasion, but I do recall that Bronwen was there even though she was not yet married to Bill. Bronwen was the daughter of a judge and had been a model in Paris. Bill always rather meanly said she could make a Molyneux dress look like a Marks & Spencer number just by wearing it. He was the only one who thought so: the couturier Pierre Balmain, who had designed dresses for Mae West, Brigitte Bardot and Sophia Loren, considered her one of the most beautiful woman he had ever met.

We saw in the New Year of 1962 at Cliveden. Although the key events that would make up what became known as the Profumo affair had already taken place – John Profumo and Christine Keeler having met at Cliveden in the summer of 1961 – we had no idea then of what was to descend on them all. Rumours first began swirling in 1962, and by the following New Year the whole thing was about to become a very public scandal, but in the meantime we had an idyllic, picture-perfect family New Year in the snow. Adam remembers being pulled, age six, by horse on a toboggan. It wasn't so much a toboggan as an open sled – a few planks of wood bound together, on which the children lay flat – pulled terrifically fast by a pony down slopes and round corners. You couldn't have got me anywhere near it. I'd never seen anything so dangerous in all my life. Adam's other main entertainment was travelling up and down in the lift. He also, to my shame, headbutted Lady Astor. History does not record why.

After the Profumo affair had broken, I felt very sorry for Bill. He had been an innocent host – and a jolly good one. The press were trying to make him look dirty but he wasn't. Neither was he strong like his mother. Nancy Astor, the first woman to sit in the House of Commons, had always been such a powerful character, and she pushed and pushed and pushed him. I remember the scene when he had opened a hospital for the Canadians just near Cliveden. He had stood on a soap box to make his speech and his mother had made unhelpful remarks all the way through. Afterwards, he came off the thing and I was standing quite near and heard him say to her, 'Mother, won't you let me do one thing properly by myself.' He was never going to be able to live up to her. Now – not that anybody took any notice of what I did, I was a nobody, after all – I remained loyal to poor Bill.

As well as my son, husband and friends, I was also blessed during my time at The Leys with two wonderful dogs. After Sherry had been run over on our first day at the school, we got a new long-haired dachshund, Sugar, and a Boxer, Samba. Samba never hurt anybody in her life, but one day she came in useful as a kind of attack dog. Barker was away, on a world tour visiting current boys' families and drumming up business for the school. It was evening, almost dark, and out of the windows I saw that a gang of teenage boys from the town had somehow got into the school grounds and were making their way towards one of the boys' houses – a fairly newly-built one that was rather distant from the others. They were singing loudly, probably drunk. Then they started shouting up to the boys, 'Come on out and fight.' I rang up the deputy head and told him he'd better come quickly. Then I put Samba on a lead and advanced across the playing field, bellowing, 'Stand back, men. She bites.' In fact, Samba just thought she was going for a lovely surprise walk, and her tail was wagging like mad, but because Boxers don't really have tails, just a stump, the boys couldn't see that. Between us we absolutely terrorized them and they all ran away.

I always got the best veterinary attention for my dogs, because the vet at Cambridge University was greatly indebted to me. I had managed to persuade a friend to donate a great deal of money to the university to fund a veterinary fellowship there, and so I only had to ring the vet and he came. That was very important to me, as you might imagine. One day my long-haired dachshund and my Boxer went out on their own and came back dragging a toad and looking absolutely extraordinary. Their faces had puffed right up. I rang the vet and said, 'Ha ha ha, I can't tell you how funny the dogs look.' He said, 'I'm on my way. I'm coming straight round.' He arrived and took one look and injected each of them before telling me how lucky I had been. The toad's venom was not only slowly causing their faces to puff up but also their windpipes. Fairly soon their airways would have become completely blocked.

*

I was very contented being a mother and headmaster's wife, but that didn't fully occupy my energies, so I embarked on a couple of little sidelines, all rather born of necessity.

Many of my friends had nothing but beautiful things whereas I had absolutely no money of my own. I used to rack my brains to think of what I could give them as presents. One day I hit upon the idea of making cushions mounted with representations of their houses worked in needlepoint. The first one I did, of Michael Edwards' house in Provence, was pretty pitiful compared with my later efforts. I hadn't at that point worked out how to do the windows. But I became very good at it and even my most sophisticated friends loved them.

I also became best pals with the owners of all the antique shops again, just like I had in Eton, and managed to make some money from buying and selling. Some of the owners were great characters. The man who owned the funny little antique shop Gabor Cossa opposite the Fitzwilliam was, I think, Hungarian. He once gave a silent concert. He invited a hundred people into a hall where he sat down at a grand piano with nothing in it and spent three-quarters-of-an-hour playing – but not a sound, not a sound did he make. At the end he got a standing ovation. It was ridiculous.

My other sideline was appearing in television quiz shows. I had first started to make some money out of quiz shows when I had been in New York. I'd had no money then either, and it was a rather jolly way of making some. My first ever appearance had been in September 1952, when I was picked out of an audience on an all-in wrestling show. 'Remember: the nation's top wrestlers are on Channel 9, Saturdays, 8.30.' I didn't wrestle, you may be pleased to hear. They asked me questions, I answered them, and I won a prize, which I sold. I can't remember what the prize was on that particular show but it was usually enormous things like deep freezes or fridges.

I had a trick to help me get picked, because there were always three or four hundred people in the television audience, all wanting to be on the telly, all wanting to be on the show. I always wore a hat, and white gloves, and I always made whichever chap came with me wear a bow tie. So when they said, 'Who wants to be on the show?' I would put up my hands, both of them. And they would say, 'The lady with the white gloves, sitting next to the gentleman in the bow tie.' It was entirely my own idea and it always worked.

Back in England, I carried on, still sporting my white gloves, and in 1960 I went on *Take Your Pick* and won an entire bedroom suite, which I flogged immediately because we had no room for it. Then, in 1971 I went on an antiques quiz show called *Going for a Song*, a quiz about antiques which I loved. When it came to antiques I really did know what I was talking about. The programme pitted two teams against one another with each having to guess how much things were worth, and when they dated from and so on. My team won, and they gave me a jolly nice old box of games – ancient playing cards and mother-of-pearl bridge counters and so on – made from a rich coromandel wood and lined with purple silk. It was so lovely that for once I didn't sell it. I still have it to this day.

Apart from quiz shows, I also undertook some more serious work. In the late 1950s I became a governor of the local mother and baby home, which was based in a big Edwardian house just opposite the school. These don't exist now, I'm pleased to say. At the time they took in single girls who had become pregnant, gave them somewhere to deliver their babies, and then immediately removed the babies and put them up for adoption. East Anglia was full of air force and army bases at the time and perhaps as a consequence there were a lot of single girls with illegitimate babies. The woman who ran the home was a good woman, but stern. I felt so sorry for these girls, who usually had no education and no background and couldn't really stand up to someone like her. I took Adam to a garden party in aid of the home once and a small boy aged about five came up to me and asked, 'Have you got any more at home?'

'No,' I said, pointing at Adam, 'he's the only one.'

'Well I expect you send the others away to good homes,' came the response. Poor little chap; it was pathetic. In the true, heartbreaking sense of that word. These children knew that they had brothers and sisters who had been taken away. And it seems to me that the damage that was done then goes on and on.

Over the years I built up my voluntary work. I served on the United Cambridge Hospital Board, the Social Services Committee and the Cambridge Folk Museum Committee. I was a member of the Rheumatism and Arthritis Association and chair of Cambridge Guide Dogs for the Blind.

Then, in the early 1970s I became a magistrate. This was around the time of the Cambridge Rapist. He attacked numerous women, threatening them with a knife, and the police were desperate to catch him but were pretty stumped. The police had said to me that an incredible number of wives in Cambridge had rung in to say they thought their husbands could have done it. At the time I used to have a Mac Fisheries man come on Fridays with fish and veg and whatever I needed for weekend entertaining. The Mac Fisheries man would drop off all my groceries and I would always say, 'Must lock the door after you've gone in case the Cambridge Rapist comes.' When they finally caught the wretched man, I was the sitting magistrate. They brought up the prisoner, but it wasn't anyone's husband – it was my Mac Fisheries delivery man. I had to leave the bench straight away of course.

I never dreamt, when I first started volunteering locally, what it would eventually lead to. But it is undoubtedly true that throughout this happy period of my life, I became more and more interested in, and more and more involved in, politics.

CHAPTER TWELVE

Political Beginnings

Politics and politicians had always been in my life, from childhood. As I've said, my father really did know Lloyd George – as did my mother – and I, of course, was his one and only land girl. But even without that illustrious connection, I think I would always have been interested in politics. During the war one didn't really think politically – at least I didn't, I just thought about getting on with the war and winning it – but after the war I became involved again, canvassing in the 1945 general election for Bill Astor. That was my first conscious political act, I suppose. The important thing when knocking on doors, I realized, was to be invited in, especially in the multi-storey blocks of flats that made up a large part of Bill's Fulham constituency. Any conversation that took place on the doorstep could be overheard by the neighbours, so people wouldn't talk to you out there at all. I worked out a very good method. At the first few flats, I would ask for a glass of water. 'I'm terribly sorry,' I would say, 'but it's frightfully hot. Do you think I could possibly have a glass of water?' They would invite me in and get me a glass of water and that would take time, and in the meantime we could have a conversation. After a few flats, I changed my line. 'I am terribly sorry, but I've been drinking so much water. Could I possibly come in and use the loo?' And in I would go. And another conversation. It may have taken more time, but I got truthful answers from them. The moment you were inside people talked to you in a way they never would on the doorstep. And I found I loved doing it.

I was amongst politicians again when I worked for Hinch, but after that years passed during which I had very little to do with politics, local or national. When we moved to Cambridge in 1958 I joined the local Conservative Party and revived my canvassing skills. Barker immediately became active, too, supporting the general election campaign of our local MP, Sir Hamilton Kerr. Ham became devoted to Barker and me, and through him we met lots of terrifically interesting Conservative people: Selwyn Lloyd, Rab Butler, Francis Pym, Irene Ward, Peter Thorneycroft, Enoch Powell. Many of them became our good friends. Powell wasn't one of those, but I do remember him as utterly charming. He told me that on his wedding day, he had given his new wife a red rose. Every wedding anniversary, he continued to give her red roses, with one flower to mark each year of their marriage. He also said that it had now become frightfully expensive, as they had been married so long. But what a lovely thing to do.

It was at Ham's that we got to know Harold Macmillan, too. It turned out that his daughter had a house in Sandwich Bay as well, so Macmillan used to come to dinner with us at Luckboat House when he was visiting her. He was an autocratic old bastard but what no one realized was that he was in constant pain. He'd been wounded in his back during the First World War and it troubled him for the rest of his life.

It was luck, or accident, that I ever became a councillor: because, really, what had I done in my life? Nothing. But a couple of years after we moved to Cambridge, I went to my first ever Trumpington Conservative Association annual general meeting. The main business of the meeting was choosing a candidate to become the local city councillor for Trumpington, which was the area of Cambridge on the road from London made up of Trumpington Town and Trumpington Village. There were two old men there, fighting endlessly as to which of them it should be. I leant over and whispered to the woman sitting next to me that I had a jolly good mind to put my own name forward just to keep the peace. The next thing I knew, my neighbour was on her feet, saying,

'Mrs Barker would be delighted to stand.' And there I was: I was the candidate. I then, of course, canvassed as though my life depended on it. One old man who had voted Labour all his life voted for me because I admired his dahlias so effusively. On the day itself, I drove pensioners to the polling station all day. Two of them particularly stick in my memory. I wasn't sure how on the ball they were so I kept saying all the way there in the car, 'Vote Barker, vote Barker.' In they went. When they got back in the car, they said, 'Well, we didn't like any of their names, so we crossed them out and put Mr Macmillan.' They got a pretty rough ride home. But it all worked out. I was a councillor and would remain one for the next ten years.

I somehow managed to get myself onto all the committees that most interested me – both inside and outside the council – and I learnt such a lot. I sat on the board of Addenbrookes Hospital and the board of an approved school and I was a governor of two secondary schools. I learnt about all the hospitals, about the health service, about housing and about the police force. I was a great supporter of the police – and they of me. I used to have to park my car in a multistorey car park and it was one of those dark, smelly car parks where you are never quite sure what is going to happen or who you are going to meet. The police gave me a truncheon, quite illegally. Heaven knows what they imagined I would actually do with it. I still have it, hanging in my hallway. Which again, is illegal, because it's an offensive weapon. They could come and arrest me for that, right now.

I also pulled off a tremendous fundraising coup. I persuaded the Cambridge Arts Theatre to give me its takings for one night. I didn't even have to work that hard to persuade them, actually: I just don't think anyone had thought of asking before. Then I persuaded the Cambridge Footlights to perform on the charity night, and we sold the place out – 500 seats at £1 a ticket. That was a lot of money in those days. What was even better was that quite by chance, the night I had picked ended up being the night of the general election. It gave the Footlights plenty of material. The county and the city MPs turned up – both Conservatives – and sat in the front row, where they were given a standing ovation. I don't suppose that could happen now, but back then MPs did command a certain respect. I made an appeal on stage in my best evening dress. It was quite a night.

*

I know Barker would have liked to have had a political career himself and he did indeed toy with the idea of the House of Commons. But that was never an option for us financially: the Cambridge seat was still quite marginal so there was a risk that he would give up his job to become an MP then lose the seat four years later. I also don't think he would have liked campaigning and canvassing: he once said that if there had still been rotten boroughs he would have tried to get someone to give him one of those. He did become a county alderman but that was as far as it went.

In many ways he would have been a terrific politician – perhaps even a better politician than he was a headmaster. The one problem would have been his unwillingness to compromise. It is difficult to be a politician if you can't compromise.

So Barker focused his ambitions elsewhere and in 1969, when we had been at The Leys for eleven years, Barker applied to become headmaster at Eton. It was the job he had always desperately wanted. He had applied once before, in 1963, and had just been beaten by Anthony Chenevix-Trench. Chenevix-Trench had not been considered a complete success, and many masters ended up regretting that Barker hadn't been given it.

However, I was well aware that that did not mean he was bound to get the job this second time around. Barker had been something of a troublemaker and rabble-rouser when he had been a young beak at Eton and this had not been forgotten. Whether Barker knew it or not, he still had enemies. I knew this. I also felt that, although Barker had been a terrific headmaster at The Leys, it didn't automatically follow that he would be right for Eton. I felt he was too clever, too original and too much of a reformer: his ideas would have been considered dangerous. And he would have had terrible rows with the very same masters with whom he had colluded and politicked all those years ago.

Barker, though, was more confident than I was and I had to let him make his own decisions. He had been offered the headship at Westminster School – where our friend Rab Butler was chair of governors – but turned them down in anticipation of getting the headship at Eton. It was not to be, however. The job went to a man called Michael McCrum (who later not only became a great friend of Barker's but also gave a wonderful eulogy at his memorial service). Not getting the Eton job was a tragedy for Barker, and one he never really recovered from. I think the iron entered his soul then. He knew he would never get what he really, really wanted and the disappointment consumed him. From that point on, there was a part of him that stopped caring.

*

At almost the same time as Barker suffered this grave disappointment, I was made Mayor of Cambridge. It was a largely ceremonial office and the political parties took turns to nominate its holders. I suppose the party picked me because I had been a good girl. I'd been asked to do lots of public things, and I'd said yes willingly and thrown myself into them, and I suppose done them competently. None of it was really done with a particular plan in mind, it was just that when I was asked to do something, I did it. I do always say now to young people who want to go into politics that you've got to be prepared to say yes to a lot of boring things to get what you want.

I took up the mayoralty on 27 May 1971, having been installed in ancient ceremonial at the Cambridge Guildhall. I adored being mayor. I loved the dressing up and pageantry: the scarlet robes, the splendid black velvet hat, the gold chain, the mace and so on. The chain was encrusted with diamonds and emeralds, and ruinous of my clothes because it was so heavy. I eventually came up with an ingenious solution: backing the chain with yellow velvet and fixing it into place with two nappy pins. The mace had originally been a club to hit people with, to protect the mayor. These days there is a lot of folderol at one end of it that has been put there to jazz it up, but the other end – the simple end – is the business end and it could do a lot of damage. Mine was eighteenth century and made of gold: very heavy and very beautiful. It was carried at all times by the Sergeant at Mace, a Mr Quick, who had been at the job for ages and knew everything about it, and every trick of the trade. Mr Quick and the mace came everywhere with me, including to the Midsummer Fair. There was I in full regalia squashed into one dodgem, and there was a top-hatted Mr Quick squashed into the dodgem behind me. There was me on a painted horse on the merry-go-round, and there was Mr Quick and the mace following right behind. Mr Quick swiftly became a very important person in my life.

As well as the dressing up, there was also a huge amount of opening things, and making speeches, and judging competitions, and lunching and dining: 290 functions in 365 days. I hugely enjoyed opening things – especially the Elizabeth Bridge, which I opened with Rab Butler, who was then High Steward of the City of Cambridge; and the new travel centre and entrance hall at Cambridge railway station, which I opened having arrived on the footplate of the engine of the 10.23 from Ely. I loved judging competitions, including the Miss Anglia competition: I was the first mayor ever to accept that invitation. I also gradually became reconciled to the terrifying trial of speech-making. But the lunching I could have done without. The very worst bit of it was the three weeks running up to Christmas. Every single day I ate turkey, sausages, roast potatoes, Brussels sprouts and Christmas pudding for lunch, Christmas cake and mince pies for tea and then turkey, sausages, roast potatoes and so on for supper. Every day.

It was also my job to chair the meetings of fifty-four councillors and aldermen in the council chamber. I loved Mr Quick forever after the occasion when I was stuck in a long and hot council meeting late at night, overheating terribly in my robes, and he, with huge dignity, marched in with a silver salver and a full glass. Thinking it was water, I took a huge gulp, and it was pure gin. He was quite right, though; it was just what I needed.

Being mayor may not have been a political role but I did try to use it to do some things that I thought were important.

I resurrected the town market, in the ancient centre of the city. The square overlooked by the Guildhall that had hosted markets since the Middle Ages had become a car park and I was determined to return it to its proper use. As always with anything to do with parking, it provoked great outrage and made me very unpopular for a while. But the market brought bustle and life to the centre of the city. Before long people realized how much they preferred seeing the stalls selling home-grown vegetables and books and shoes and the odd antique, instead of parked cars.

I also managed to persuade Cambridge to give the Freedom of the City to the RAF. Cambridge was surrounded by a great many air fields and at the end of the Second World War, the Freedom of the City had been given to the American air force, but it had never been given to the RAF at Oakington, which caused terrible upset. Thirty-odd years later I got it through. On the day of the ceremony, I stood on a platform with the lord lieutenant, taking the salute as the Queen's Colour Squadron and the Support Squadron – hundreds of men – marched by, with swords drawn, bayonets fixed, bands playing and colours flying. There was a fly past, a tea and then a party. I remember lying on the floor, quite drunk and blind-folded, with the squadron leader and a lot of other airmen. We were playing a game of some sort. I can't begin to remember how it worked now, but it involved banging about with folded-up newspapers and a lot of screaming. You had to call out, 'Where am I, sister Anne?' It was a hoot!

I was very keen, as mayor, to support charitable activities, too, and launched two great appeals: one for the India and Pakistan Relief Fund to help the millions of people affected by the terrible Indo-Pakistani War, and another for Addenbrooke's Hospital, which was then under construction. The hospital was being built out of town and there was nowhere for the doctors and nurses working there to go to relax. The appeal was for £100,000, to build a recreation centre and it was particularly dear to my heart because it was going to be named after our great friend Frank Lee, whose original idea it had been, as a memorial to him. I worked very hard writing to everyone I knew asking for donations and the most wonderful thing happened. One person I appealed to had pots of money, but he turned me down. Three weeks later, I received a letter from his wife. 'I was going through my husband's waste paper basket and I found your letter. I like nurses. Would £10,000 be of any help?'

I decided to lead by example by taking part in a sponsored swim in aid of commendable local charities, launching the swim by breast-stroking the first length, with the town clerk acting as the mayor's escort. There were mutterings of disapproval that it might tarnish the dignity of the office. As a result, on the day some frightfully high-up official was on hand with a huge towel at the beginning of the swim so that nobody could see me get into the water. At the other end of the pool was my dentist, holding another huge towel. So nobody saw me in my bathing suit and the dignity of the office was preserved intact. And we raised a lot of money.

I was also very lucky to go on three foreign visits; to Florence, for the opening of an extraordinary Henry Moore exhibition – smooth black figures set amongst the Tuscan hills, with the red-orange of the Duomo in the background; to Cambridge's twin town of Heidelberg;

and, most eventfully, to the beautiful Roman city of Split, in Yugoslavia as it was then, representing Cambridge at a conference for historic European towns. Thrillingly, my friend John Henniker, who had seen action in Yugoslavia during the war, gave me an introduction to the general who had led the underground movement at the time. Less thrillingly, I was suddenly informed at a big dinner that I was expected to make a speech. I had nothing prepared and was absolutely terrified but somehow I stumbled my way through it. The next day I wandered around the town looking for a particular kind of wine that Barker liked. I was in the shop trying to make myself understood when a very good-looking woman heard me struggling away and helped me out. I offered her a drink that evening at my hotel in return. Along she came, and was a great hit with all the old men from every country who had gathered for this conference.

*

Barker was supportive of my political career, up to a point. I think he was proud of me, though he would never have told me so. But he never helped me financially, not even to pay the £65 for me becoming a candidate. I don't know whether it was jealousy, or just that he felt as a matter of principle that I ought to stand on my own two feet, because I remember he said, 'If you want to do it you have got to do it, but I want nothing to do with it.' As I had no income of my own, and as I helped him so much with his job, I rather resented that. But we never discussed it any further. I certainly wasn't going to beg him. So I scraped the money together from buying and selling antiques and quiz show prizes.

Once I became mayor, Barker didn't ever much like playing second fiddle to me either. It's pretty difficult for a man to take second place to his wife. Dinners were difficult because I had my place at the head of the table and he would have to wander around the room searching for his name. He became particularly incensed at the rules around the mayoral car: if I wasn't in the car, the mayoral flag came off, and he was driven home in a flagless car. I decided not to make him mayoress, I thought that might make things worse.

Adam, at the age of sixteen, probably felt pretty ambivalent about the whole thing too – half-proud, half-ashamed. I think the time I shamed him most completely was on Christmas Eve when I was reading one of the lessons in the Festival of Nine Lessons and Carols at King's College Chapel. It is such a beautiful and moving service it defies belief. The service begins with a single choirboy singing the first verse of 'Once in Royal David's City', which is heart-stoppingly wonderful. I thought I had read my lesson about the lion and the lamb quite exquisitely but when I came to sit down Adam leant over and whispered, 'Mum, trust you to think of food.' Apparently I had said, 'the little lamb shall feed them' instead of 'the little lamb shall lead them'. I was terribly embarrassed.

The boys at The Leys were, by contrast, simply very sweet about my political office. When I'd become mayor they sent me a card signed by each and every one of them, saying, 'Of course you can eat like a horse, but now you're a mare.'

One is mayor for a year and then it is someone else's turn. At the end of my term of office, I commissioned a grand and beautiful goblet for Barker, to say thank you for being Mr Mayor. What I didn't know was that friends of ours had commissioned an identical goblet, but with our initials engraved on it, for the two of us. Although they made a perfect pair, my own present was entirely overshadowed and I was actually very upset.

*

After I left office, I realized I had enjoyed my time as mayor so much that I wanted to remain in politics. I decided to try to stand for parliament.

As a good headmaster's wife I could only try for local seats. And East Anglia, back then, didn't like women, and was certainly not ready for me. I couldn't even get selected. I got as far as the shortlist for the Isle of Ely –

a godforsaken bit of the world, albeit with a lovely cathedral – but the panel clearly hadn't even bothered to read my CV and called me Mrs Baker all through the interview. I was too frightened and nervous to correct them. At the end, they said, 'Why do you think there are so few women in parliament?' By this time I knew I wasn't going to make it so I said, 'Because of selection committees like you.' I walked out of the room and burst into tears. They chose a Dr Thomas Stuttaford instead, who lost out in the election to the Liberal, Clement Freud.

By the mid-seventies, therefore, both Barker and I were blissfully happy at home, but disappointed professionally. I had tried and failed to become an MP. He had tried and failed to become headmaster of Eton. What we couldn't possibly have known was that Barker's career was nearly over while mine had barely begun.

CHAPTER THIRTEEN

And Then . . .

My life has been divided into two parts: my life as a wife and my life since, in which the House of Lords has filled the huge gap that Barker left. This book is really about the first half of my life, not about the ins and outs of my ministerial career: those with a particular interest can read Hansard. But there must be at least one chapter devoted to my second life, which in its way has been as full of incident and excitement, and certainly as full of kindness, as was my first.

In 1975, after seventeen happy years in Cambridge, Barker and I moved to Hampstead in North London, where Barker took up a position as headmaster of University College School. Running a day school presented a new challenge, and one that Barker was ready for. Tragically though, soon after we arrived, a terrible fire destroyed great parts of the school. As a result Barker spent his first few years there managing its aftermath. The strain undoubtedly took its toll.

I was not bored: as well as being the headmaster's wife at UCS, I was on the Board of Visitors of HM Prison Pentonville, a member of the Mental Health Review Tribunal, a commissioner of taxes, a member of the Air Transport Users' Committee and a magistrate. I kept up with my old friends and met some new fascinating people, including Harold Wilson and his lovely wife Mary, whose sons were pupils at UCS. The Wilsons came to lunch twice and of course I invited all the other VIPs I could find, and he sat in a chair and he held court. It was less of a lunch, more of a meeting.

But, just like my father when I was a girl, Barker now went around saying to various people, 'You've got to do something about Jean.' And I think his friends Peter Thorneycroft and Rab Butler agreed. I'm sure it was their doing that, in 1980, Margaret Thatcher made me a life peer. It certainly had nothing to do with me.

When one is made a lord, one is given a coat of arms and a motto, and of course a new name. My coat of arms has a Boxer dog rampant on one side and a racing filly rampant on the other. And then three hedgehogs, because the French word for hedgehog is '*un hérisson*', and the Pursuivant of Arms discovered that my maiden name, Campbell-Harris, had originally been Herries. For my motto, I chose '*gagne tout, sans atout*'. It's French for 'win all, no trumps'. Which I often think is absolutely what I've done. The name – Baroness Trumpington of Sandwich in the County of Kent – made no sense at all, but was a quite deliberate combination of the two places I considered home and had the added advantage that Trumpington sounds rather splendid.

I was introduced into the Lords by Rab and Peter, with Rab moaning like mad about how much it had cost him to get his robes and chains and so on for the day. (That was just like Rab. I remember once at dinner he bellowed to his wife, all the way down at the other end of the table, 'What am I going to say to this woman you've sat me next to?' Tact was not his strong point.) We processed in behind Black Rod, wearing parliamentary robes and special tri-corner hats – like Wren officers' hats – and proceeded to stand in front of the Lord Chancellor sitting on the Woolsack. Then there was a great deal of ceremony during which time I was supposed to go down on one knee. I knew if I did that I would never get up so I did a sort of sweeping bow of my own creation. We were then led to our seats, right at the back of the cross-benchers' pew. At various moments we all three then had to put on our hats, stand up, doff our hats and bow to the Lord Chancellor, and then we processed back out again and the whole place cheered. My robes were too long and therefore terribly dangerous up and down all those stairs. I was very nervous of a disastrous or, worse, an embarrassing fall.

Then it was time for my maiden speech, which was also rather a traumatic occasion. Back then – different from now, when it is done as a show-piece – you tried to sneak it in when nobody would hear you and get the thing over with, and of course that is exactly what I aimed for. My family all turned up and sat in the gallery, and then suffered through an awful lot of waiting for my golden words while the debate went on and on. Eventually, at eight o'clock at night, I stood up. I wanted to say something about housing for the elderly: I had done a lot of work on this as a councillor and I knew what the main problems were. So I banged on about old people's homes and I talked about a rather inelegant but important subject: incontinence, and the need for proper facilities to deal with it. It wasn't a glamorous maiden speech but I didn't care. I was convinced that I had a terribly important point to make, a point that had hitherto gone unrecognized. As I got going into my speech, everyone began to laugh. I was terribly upset, but I ploughed on. It wasn't until afterwards that I discovered that as I had been discussing in detail the council's lavatories the heavens had opened, and all anyone could hear was rushing water. Then it was off for dinner and a hell of a party, given by my brother David.

I quickly came to adore the Lords. I had to be very careful before I spoke in the Chamber because make one mistake in that place and you get shot down in an elegant but vicious way. Despite that, I found the House to be a kind place with a very special atmosphere. I thoroughly enjoyed mixing with those wonderful experts. I was terribly lucky because I won the ballot for a debate very early on and chose to talk about shop opening hours. I then found myself piloting a private member's bill on the same subject. What sense was there in a law that said a mother could buy a bottle of gin on a Sunday but not milk for her baby? Or a newspaper from a newsagent but not a Bible from a bookshop? The law was simply outdated. Later I was made a privy councillor, which was an immense honour.

I'm afraid I have never been a very well-behaved lord. I have always been too apt to say exactly what I thought. Once there was a very boring Liberal speech going on and I leant across to a Lord of Appeal and said – I thought quietly – 'If I could advise anybody, now is the time to go and have a pee.' And do you know, he stood up, and I nearly fainted. He said, 'Well, if I am given good advice, I take it.' What bliss! A Lord of Appeal. It doesn't get grander. And, of course, when my good friend Tom King commented that those people who had served in the Second World War were starting to look 'pretty old', it was a natural reaction to stick two fingers up at him. I had thought it was between him and me, but the camera was on me, so it was between him, me and everyone who had a computer or a television. At first I tried to say I had just been primping my hair but when I looked at the film it was perfectly obvious what I was doing so I had to admit to it.

That was probably what got me picked for *Have I Got News for You*. I rather think they saw me making that naughty gesture and thought I might be an amusing guest. I hope I was amusing. I started off before we'd even really got going by asking why, as a ninety-year-old woman, I had been asked to fill in a health and safety form to say that I was not pregnant, and it went from there. I certainly enjoyed teasing Jack Whitehall, who is a lovely young man.

As well as saying just what I thought, I always liked making people laugh in the Lords, which sometimes caused bad behaviour – or at least behaviour considered rather unusual in the House. Once I got up to remind the House that I had once been Lloyd George's land girl and they all screamed with laughter, which I hadn't really meant them to do. But the next day a minister started talking about Emperor Claudius. Finally I couldn't bear it any longer, so I stood up and when the minister gave way I said, 'I just wanted, my Lords, to inform the Speaker that

I was not the Emperor Claudius' land girl.' I couldn't resist. On the other hand, if you want to get a serious message over to people – which I did, a lot of the time – it's no bad thing to make them laugh if you possibly can. It means taking a bit of a chance, but it's worth trying, because once you've made them laugh once, they keep listening, in case you say something funny again. In between the jokes you can slip in the message you want them to receive.

*

Two years after I went to the Lords, in 1982, I was spending the evening at the Cavalry Club, with Jackie d'Avigdor-Goldsmid, while Barker was at a headmaster's affair somewhere else in London. Jackie was a lovely eternal bachelor and had hired out the Double Bridal Room for the evening, which was a private dining suite decorated with racing memorabilia. One always thought it should be the Double Bridle Room but it wasn't, it was named after the racehorse Double Bridal. There were eight of us there for dinner and bridge and I was standing around being jolly with everyone before dinner when the door-bell rang. There were two headmasters standing at the door. They told us that they had been at the dinner with Barker and that, in the middle of dinner, he had had a stroke. He had been taken to Westminster Hospital and the headmasters were going to drive me over there. 'Oh,' said one of the guests. 'Who's going to make up the eight for bridge?'

When I saw Barker he was stretched out in one of those hospital bays with a curtain around it, and the first thing he said to me was, 'Take my watch, somebody will nick it otherwise.' I thought, well he can't be that bad. And it was true that he hadn't lost his marbles at all. But he couldn't move. The stroke had left him paralysed down one side, and the other side was the leg that had been shot in the war. He never walked again.

Adam was by this time living and working in New York, where our old friend John Lindsay had given him a job in his law firm. John happened to be in London when Barker had his stroke and not only visited him straight away but then got on a plane back to New York so that he could break the news to Adam.

The stroke was Barker's second tragedy (not getting the Eton job was the first) and I fear it rather finished him. I do believe that he never really tried to get better. He used to lie on the floor when everyone else was doing their exercises and do nothing. There was no point my saying anything, it wouldn't have made a blind bit of difference. So instead I went backwards and forwards, backwards and forwards to the hospital, which was being turned upside down with all of Barker's visitors: the foreign secretary Douglas Hurd and various other distinguished former pupils came to see him, and every time the whole ward was tidied up to make it respectable. And to each of them, Barker said, 'Jean is the best thing that ever happened to me.'

Barker eventually accepted that he would have to leave the headmaster's job at UCS. This, in turn, meant we were homeless again. We decided that Barker should live permanently down at Luckboat House, in Sandwich, and that I should live in a flat in London so that I could be in the Lords during the week, and travel down to Sandwich at weekends. It was tough on both of us: lonely for Barker, who suddenly found himself confined to a wheelchair and living in what was in effect a holiday home, and exhausting for me. We also had to give away our beloved Boxer dog, Bumble, because I couldn't look after a dog and a husband and try to earn some money. It was a pretty dreadful time.

The flat I found was on Cundy Street near Sloane Square. There are four or five blocks of perfectly nice but rather small flats there, on land owned by the Duke of Westminster. When the duke was taken to see one of the blocks, as they were being completed, he asked, 'What is this cupboard?' 'That, your Grace,' replied one of his retinue, 'is the flat.' The duke said that every flat must be made four feet larger, which made quite a difference in a small flat and worked out to my benefit. But after living in the headmaster's house for the last twenty years, whether at The Leys or UCS, even the bigger flat felt small to me.

The flats might have been tiny, but they were conveniently close to Westminster and many politicians lived in the same building, including Alec Douglas-Home. Once, when I had done something good, Margaret Thatcher came through to thank me. I can't for the life of me remember what it was, but I seized the moment and said, 'Couldn't you please get Lord Home to take a government car?' I couldn't understand why he hadn't got one, because if you've been a prime minister you have a free government car with driver for life.

'We've tried,' she said, 'but he won't do it.'

'No,' I said, 'because he knows I will drive him home.' In a tiny little Ford: a sort of van that I'd had adapted for Alan. I don't know how Alec got himself up to the Lords, but I used to take him home almost every night.

In 1983, following the general election, Margaret Thatcher asked me to join her government and become a whip. I hesitated. I tried to phone Barker to ask him – I was still a good wife, I always asked permission – but he was out at dinner at our neighbours' in Sandwich and didn't answer. Adam was still living in New York. It fell to an old Leysian called Sir Percy Rugg to advise me, and he urged me to take the job. He told me that Barker would enjoy seeing me outside Downing Street more than he would seeing me do his laundry.

Thus began a rewarding but stressful and guilt-inducing time. I was a government whip during the week, and continuing to work hard on getting my Sunday trading bill through. No one realized but I suffered dreadfully with nerves every time I was at the Dispatch Box. (It was the Labour Party chief whip who took me aside and gave me some tips, saying, 'We girls must stick together.' I paid that kindness back fifteen years later, doing the same thing for the new Labour whips in 1997.) At weekends I went down to Sandwich with my red boxes, getting the work done after I had put Alan to bed. I was lucky I had such a strong constitution. Even so, after a couple of years of trying to manage – and not entirely succeeding – we all decided it would be better if Barker moved to the Royal Star & Garter Home in Richmond. Thankfully, he was much happier there and I was less exhausted, but a bit of me died when we sold Luckboat House.

Barker lived another three years after that. He made it to Adam's wedding to Elizabeth Marsden in Stourpaine, Dorset (which had rather an Etonian aspect to it as they had met through Ronnie Furse and two of Elizabeth's uncles had been beaks), and to the christening of their first child, Virginia, in the Chapel of St Mary Undercroft. We gave up the Cundy Street flat and with the capital from Luckboat House bought a bigger ground-floor flat in Battersea that had a little garden for me and would be easier for Barker to manage when he came at weekends. Then, one morning, the phone rang. It was the matron of the Star & Garter. Barker had tormented this woman by being terribly outspoken and rude to her. He used to greet her every morning with a: 'Morning, Matron. Who are you making miserable today?' It didn't help him to make friends. 'Are you by yourself?' she now asked. I told her I was. 'Well,' she said, 'your husband's just died.' So I think she had her revenge.

*

I missed Barker terribly, and miss him still. But work helped. It gave me a sense of purpose. By this time I had been promoted again: in 1985 Mrs Thatcher made me a minister in the Department for Health and Social Security and then in 1987, after the election, she moved me to the Ministry of Agriculture, which as you can imagine I just adored. Every time I went out into the country I learnt something new and saw something beautiful – a lot of it created by our farmers. As the oldest member of the government I regarded myself as the female equivalent of Lester Piggott. I felt terribly lucky to have a job, and a job I adored, and looking back I think that at times, at least, I didn't do it too badly.

I was a minister for ten years and my career owes more to Mrs Thatcher than to anybody. She put me in the Lords; she gave me a job; and she was terribly kind to me. Once I had to attend a full cabinet because my boss wasn't able to be there, and I was terribly nervous. I just had one thing to say, which was that 'Professor So-And-So should get the job. The Secretary of State agrees.' In my terror, I said it three times. When the meeting was over she came up to me, patted me on the shoulder, and said, 'I'll see that your professor gets the job.'

When she was no longer prime minister, they used to ring her up and get her to come to the House of Lords when they needed her vote. She sat on the privy coun-cillors' bench, of course, which is also where I sat. All those people she had sacked used to get up and go when they saw her coming, and I didn't like to see the ex-prime minister sitting alone, so I would go and sit with her. We didn't talk much. From time to time I would say, 'Time to go?' and she would say, 'No.' 'Time to go?' I'd say again after a bit, and she'd say, 'Too soon. Not long enough.' But eventually she would have had enough and then we would go out together. Once, as we were leaving, she kissed me, and you could have knocked me down with a feather because she was not a kissing kind of person.

I don't always say the right thing but I was very pleased with what I said in my tribute to Baroness Thatcher in the House of Lords. In particular, I was pleased that I mentioned what a beautiful woman she was. I said, 'It took a French president to appreciate that, even if his remark had a twist – but that is typically French.' President Mitterrand had said she had the eyes of Caligula and the lips of Marilyn Monroe and he got it about right.

Baroness Thatcher's funeral was an extraordinary affair. I had to restrain myself at the time – because it would have caught on – from calling it Black Ascot. But that is exactly what it was. Everybody who had ever been a cabinet minister, and all the Royals, and all the foreign dignitaries were there, and their wives: all in their hats and best jewellery, but everything in black.

They wanted me on *Have I Got News for You* when she died. I agreed to do it, but when I got there I realized they were going to use the programme to make fun of her. It seemed very clear to me that they were getting a mob up to make silly jokes about a woman who had just died and I wouldn't do it. Well, you can imagine the chaos and the fuss. They got the ex-leader of the Greater London Council instead, Ken Livingstone. Fine for him to be rude about Mrs Thatcher. Not fine for me. I think it was quite brave of me because I did have to cause a terrible scene, but sometimes you do have to stand up for something.

*

I loved being a minister. And alongside all of that excitement, partly because of my work as a councillor in Cambridge and partly as a result of becoming a lord and a minister, I found myself with all kinds of other wonderful, and occasionally rather eccentric, jobs.

One of the most fascinating was that I was made a baroness-in-waiting within the royal household. I was absolutely delighted about this – and not a little surprised, because my previous encounter with the royal family, at a private drinks party at Clarence House in the early seventies, had been slightly awkward. I had only been there as Barker's wife: he had been invited because of something to do with a book he had written on the American Civil War. It was a big thrill and a great honour because there were only a few people there. But I had a terribly delicate social situation to navigate. I had to go up to the Queen Mother and say, 'Ma'am, I'm terribly sorry, but we are dining with the Speaker and we have to go.' When you are dining with the Speaker – which I did fairly often, because we were friends and he had no wife – you have to be terribly punctual because he can only be out of the chair for half an hour. 'Having dinner with the Speaker,' said the Queen Mother. 'That's rather grand, isn't it?' Very funny, and so like her.

As a baroness-in-waiting, my main role – and one about which I can't say very much – was to greet visitors to the United Kingdom on behalf of the Queen. When people deplaned at Heathrow I would be the first person to speak to them and they would have twenty minutes with me while their passport and transport and so on was sorted out. It means there is practically no one I haven't met, but it was always especially lovely when I had to greet the King of Bahrain, because we remembered each other from when he had been a pupil at The Leys.

I always found the president of Afghanistan to be a very dignified man, but on one occasion when I met him he was in a dreadful state. His wife had just given birth to a long-awaited son. He was so thrilled about it, it was all he could talk about. After he had gone back to Afghanistan I went down to the Lords shop and discovered a lovely Bakelite set: a plate, a spoon and fork, a cup, a saucer and a bowl. It only cost 99p but it was rather sweet. I bought it and rang up the Foreign Office and asked them how I could get it to the president of Afghanistan, and they said I should bring it over and they would get it to him. Without really believing them, that is what I did. And a few weeks later I received a letter from the ambassador saying the president thought my present was the greatest thing that had ever happened, and what a great service I had done. I knew how much this baby meant to him, you see. I always felt it was one of my small contributions to good international relations.

Sometimes if people arrived very late at night they would go straight to their hotel rather than meeting the Queen straight away, and I would be sent to their suite to present the Queen's compliments. Once I found myself alone in a room with Robert Mugabe. This was soon after his first wife Sally had died. I knew Sally; she was a lovely, sweet person. (In fact I had been to visit her when she was dying in St Mary's Hospital. They had given her a pseudonym to protect her identity. Mrs Smith, they called her. They called everyone who needed a pseudonym Mrs Smith I expect but Iain Smith was Mugabe's great political opponent. When I explained the error to her kidney specialist he was mortified, but Sally and I thought it was screamingly funny.) In this hotel suite, alone with President Mugabe, who was about half my size, I said, 'I am terribly sorry, Mr President, about your wife. I would like you to know that she was a lovely person and I was very fond of her.' Silence. Can you imagine? He didn't say a word to me. He just glowered. I couldn't get out of the room fast enough.

I longed to see what a state dinner was like, and asked whether I could serve at one. I wanted to see all the gold and silver and the flowers. I was told I couldn't possibly; all the people who served at state banquets were men.

However, the royal family must have thought it was a great joke, because the next thing I knew, I had an invitation. It was the state banquet for the King of Jordan and I was seated two places down from the Queen, with the Lord Chief Justice on one side and the Jordanian prime minister on the other. What a time I had. But not everything the job entailed was such fun.

Every year, there was an annual do at the Palace for all the foreign diplomats and about 800 people went: every ambassador from every embassy, and whoever the ambassador had brought with them. The Queen went around talking to the lot of them. All the lords- and baronesses-in-waiting had to stand on the other side of the room from the diplomats and turn around and face the other way when she came in, so that it didn't look as though we were trying to attract attention. I was moving from one room to another when a man came up to me and shook me warmly by the hand and said, 'How lovely to see you.' We were very close: close enough for me to notice he had a bad eye. I had never really noticed it in photos and on the television. I looked back at him and said, 'How lovely to see *you*.' But when Gordon Brown – for it was he – heard my voice, he looked horrified; he'd obviously realized I wasn't some foreign dignitary and couldn't wait to dash off in the opposite direction.

It was at another state occasion – albeit one that I

had gatecrashed – that I met Gordon Brown's predecessor, Tony Blair. He and John Prescott had just become leader and deputy leader of the Labour Party and were therefore being made privy councillors. It's a rather tremendous ceremony: you kneel in front of the Queen and kiss her hand, and you are given a beautifully bound little New Testament with your name inscribed, and there is a lot of reading out and so forth. Then at the end the Queen has a jolly with you for a few minutes. I had done it myself several years previously. On this occasion, I had a friend who was managing director of Fortnum & Mason who was going to be made a privy councillor alongside Blair and Prescott, and he had said to me, 'I am absolutely terrified, do try to be there.' So, despite it being terribly odd, I asked whether I could go too. It was unheard of but luckily for me they said yes. So there I was. It was all most embarrassing because the Queen was trying ever so hard to make conversation and create a light atmosphere and the two Labour men never opened their mouths. So it became a dialogue between she and me. And then it was over and there was lots of curtseying and bowing, and off we all went. And still, Blair and Prescott said not a word to me. Dreadful.

Perhaps the strangest job I ever did was to represent British interests in Mongolia. I first went there in some kind of official capacity just after the collapse of the Soviet

Union back when nobody much was interested in the place. I didn't even know where Mongolia was, but off I went. The journey was terrible. I was stuck in a room at Moscow airport for hours with visa problems. Then to get to Mongolia I was put into a plane that was so small that we had to keep coming down to refuel: Omsk, Momsk, Bomsk, all the way up and all the way down again, all through the night.

The next day I was asked to make a speech – to my great surprise. I hadn't prepared anything so I said what I thought, to this room full of hundreds of people. I talked about the purity of the air and the wonderful views and apparently, because I spoke from the heart and wasn't just talking about the desperate poverty there, it went down very well. I also said that I was tired of going around government buildings and I would like to see how the people lived. That afternoon the officials hastily re-arranged my schedule and took me to a school. The teacher said to her class, 'Who would like to ask the minister a question?' Silence, then eventually up went the hand of one boy. 'Yes, stand up and ask the question,' said the teacher. So he stood up and he said, 'What's your telephone number?' Whereupon my whole Foreign Office party had hysterics.

Next stop was a ger, which is one of their traditional houses, basically an enormous portable tent with just one space where everything happens – eating, sleeping, cooking. When my hosts greeted me they were holding a blue silk scarf, which they presented to me. 'How lovely,' I said, putting it around my neck. The driver of my jeep, who luckily spoke English, said, 'Take that off at once, it is sacred, they have given you a great honour by giving it to you.' If people don't tell you, you do terrible things. I took it off immediately but I didn't know whether the damage had already been done. The lunch in the ger was awful but the fermented mare's milk was excellent.

After their revolution in 1990, Britain was the first country to recognize Mongolia. At the time it was desperately poor. Moscow had supplied it with education, health services, everything, and now that the Soviet Union had collapsed and withdrawn they had nothing. Now the Mongolians have struck copper and are hugely rich. And, because of the UK's longstanding interest and support, last year Michael Howard and I found ourselves being presented with distinguished orders at the Mongolian Embassy.

Back in 1979 I was made the UK delegate to the UN Commission on the Status of Women. That was Barker's old pupil Douglas Hurd's doing. He and Barker had adored one another but he had always been terribly shy with me. I said to him when he gave me the job, 'I do hope you haven't made a mistake here.' His reply was 'So do I,' which wasn't reassuring. There were two things I particularly loved about that job. One was that it took me back to New York. The other was that it gave me a friend in every country in the world. There was an Australian delegate I particularly liked. When she left Australia there was one party in government but halfway through the conference there was a general election and her government lost, so her briefing was entirely wrong. The result was that she came and joined the UK group and drank all our drink. The Swedes, Americans, Brits and Australians had a gorgeous time together, drinking an awful lot. But I also really rather liked the Kashmiris. You could have a giggle with them. And it was through the UN that I became friendly with Sally Mugabe. If you take trouble with people, whoever they are, you can always have a laugh and make friends.

The following year I headed up the UK delegation to the Copenhagen Conference to mark the mid-point of the UN Decade for Women, and I sat for a week doing nothing at all. On our one day off at the end of the first week, I received a message to say something very special had been laid on for me. I was terribly excited, I thought at the very least I was going to have tea with the Queen. An enormous car and chauffeur arrived for me and I was told, 'We know you are very interested in prisons, so we will take you to see a Danish prison.' My heart sank, but it was actually quite interesting: the prison had men and women in it, and they could receive visitors in their cells and have a jolly good snog. I was shocked – and I'm generally pretty unshockable.

At the beginning of the second week I sent a message to the Foreign Office through our ambassador to Denmark, Anne Warburton, who was the UK's first female ambassador and a very strong woman. She and I got on very well. 'If you don't give me something to do,' went the message, 'I am resigning in the next twenty-four hours.' I felt so stupid sitting silently for hour after hour, day after day. So they gave me something to say about people who are 'disappeared' by their governments: how many there are and what we are doing about it, that sort of thing. The other thing I did, I did off my own bat. The leader of the Egyptian delegation was Suzanne Mubarak, the half-English wife of the then Egyptian president. She made a very brave and peace-loving speech about Israel which was not sufficiently damning of the Israelis for the rest of the Arab delegations. I decided to cross the floor, which was empty and huge, to congratulate her loudly on her splendid speech. I did it very deliberately. Occasionally being six feet tall can be an asset.

One of my other jobs might sound dreadfully dull but even it came up with a thrilling moment or two. I had been a member of the Air Transport Users' Committee since 1972, and in 1979 I was made its chairman. As a result, I had one of the most exciting and certainly the hairiest experience of my life: a seat on Concorde's first flight from Heathrow to Beirut in 1975. What I remember most from the flight was the marvellous colour of the sky at that height. But Lebanon was then in the middle of a civil war. The trip had been planned in a more peaceful time but now there was no one on the plane but journalists (all men) and me. When we landed, we landed in the middle of a war zone. On the journey from the airstrip to the hotel there were gunmen shooting at each other from either side of the road. We saw the wounded coming in, bearing white flags and screaming. From my hotel bedroom window the view was of machine guns. It really taught me to admire diplomats who have to stay where they are, no matter what, at great personal risk.

We were asked, as part of the flight, to say if there was anything we thought needed changing. As the only woman on the flight, I was therefore the only one to sit down on the lavatory, and I laddered my tights on the nuts sticking out right next to it. I told them that, and they changed it. That was my contribution to Concorde.

I was also on Concorde's very last commercial flight, in October 2003. There were three planes flying simultaneously: one from New York to London, one making a round trip from Heathrow over the Bay of Biscay and the third, with me on it, making a round trip to Edinburgh and back. As we took off, the pilot said, 'Ladies and gentlemen, we are about to take off. Now, we have no luggage in this plane obviously, which means we are rather lighter than usual so you may find take-off a bit surprising.' With that, off we went. Whoosh. We were all propelled forward in a quite terrifying way. At the end of the flight, all three aircraft circled at low altitude over London then landed in sequence at Heathrow, where everyone from the pilots to the lowest bottle washer had come out onto the runway to wave goodbye. It was very moving.

I had two lovely jobs that came from my love of horses. In 1980, to my absolute joy, I was made a steward of Folkestone Racecourse. It was a surprise to them to have a woman steward and they didn't quite know how to cope with me at first. I didn't cover myself in glory at my first meet either. The senior steward, who tells the other stewards where to go for a race, told me, 'You will go to the start.' Well, the start was a mile-and-a-half away, but I wanted to do what I was told, so off I headed. Halfway there I realized I wasn't going to make it in time, so I hid behind one of the fences while the horses thundered past. When I came back the other stewards asked me, 'Well, how did you get on?' 'Well,' I said, 'I didn't make it.'

It was a good job I did admit it, because what I hadn't realized was that they had been watching me the whole time through their binoculars. 'Well now, Lady Trumpington,' said the senior steward. 'In the next race you will go to the start, but what you will do is, you will go up to the starter's car and you will say to the driver, "I am Lady Trumpington, will you please give me a lift to the start."'

'OK,' I said, and off I went to the starter's car and gave my little speech, to which the driver said, 'Certainly not, you are far too heavy, you'll ruin the going.' So I ran all the way to the start, because I was determined to make it. And I did make it. I did that job for twelve years and they gradually got used to me.

Twenty years after I was made a steward at Folkestone, in 2000, I became president of the South of England Agriculture Show for a year. It was a great honour and right up my street. I always liked to go to the floral tent, not so much because of the flowers but because they all seemed to bet like drunken sailors on the horses so we had a lot in common. We never talked about the bloody flowers, just, 'Who have you got for the 3.30?'

But I must say I did some of the stupidest things I've ever done in that job. At the time there was a great deal of trouble about hunts, and at the show there were four-teen packs of hounds and seven packs of horses. Of course I was determined to show how keen I was on hunting so into the middle of them all I walked. I got whipped to death! It was agony. All those tails wagging! But I couldn't very well run so I was stuck there.

When I finally escaped being wagged to death, I went off to see the heavy horses. I always loved the heavy horses. They were like cart horses, but posher: they were the horses that used to pull the ploughs, and before that were the mounts of the barons in armour. I always used to take them Polo Mints, because horses adore Polos. This particular time, I put out my hand with the Polos to one lovely big chap and he took them avidly and then one mint was left hanging half in, half out of his mouth. So I pushed it in. How stupid. The horse was already crunching away on the Polos and now it crunched down on my hand. God, it was agony. I thought I must have broken my finger but I didn't want anyone to know what an idiot I had been so I didn't say a word, just put my hand behind my back and carried on. But I think everyone must have known because three years later, I was at a lunch of veterinary surgeons in Sussex and a farmer walked over to me across a crowded room and said, 'My horse bit you.'

Funnily enough, the Polos came in useful at a completely different occasion. I had been sent as the government's representative to the funeral of the president of Sri Lanka, Ranasinghe Premadasa, who had been killed by a suicide bomber. I had made a silly mistake buying a black dress for it. In the Far East the colour for mourning is white, not black, so I felt very uncomfortable. They put me to stand for three hours in the sun, between Afghanistan and North Korea, before the funeral ended with the body being cast onto a pyre. Happily, I had taken a packet of Polos, which I shared with my neighbours on either side of me. Without doubt, it is the way to make political friends; North Korea and Afghanistan were far from friendly with the UK at the time, but they loved the Polos. You make friends in odd ways.

Sadly I had no Polos with me when I represented the government at former Jamaican prime minister Michael Manley's funeral. I was seated next to Fidel Castro, who had been given a rapturous reception: you could hear him approaching from the cheering in the streets, and when he came into the church everybody stood up and clapped. He was a real hero there. I must say he was a fine-looking man, but all we did was shake hands and that was it. Rather oddly, there was a woman sitting behind him who spent the entire funeral fanning him and tidying his hair.

The saddest job I ever did was serving as a prison visitor and governor at Pentonville Prison in North London. I had techniques to get the men to speak to me. We used to be taken into a big room where a load of them were mending deckchairs, and the prison officer would say,

'Anyone want to speak to the Board of Visitors?' and of course no one would move. I would walk all the way up to the far end of the room, passing everyone on my way, and a queue would form. They wanted somebody to read their letters to them, or give them advice, or they just wanted to tell someone how awful things were, but they didn't want the prison officer to hear them. I learnt a lot that way. Mostly the men were not criminals, they simply needed to learn to read and write. But it was impossible to persuade anyone to spend money on education. The saddest thing though was the way one always made dates with the prisoners to meet up with them when they came out, and they never kept them. Never. You were ready to help but you never saw them again.

Whatever the job was, whether it was at Pentonville Prison or at Buckingham Palace, I always tried my very hardest. I suppose it was partly because I felt so lucky to be doing such fascinating things. And partly, I couldn't bear the idea of anyone saying I wasn't up to the job.

*

I don't think of myself as old. But so many of my old friends are now dead. Where once it sparkled with weddings and christenings and jolly birthday parties my social life is now studded with funerals.

Saddest of all, of course, was Barker's death, in 1988.

It's hard to believe that Osla died forty years ago, while our other great friend from Bletchley, Sally, died in February 2013. Michael Edwards died in 2002, and Riv Winant, who introduced me to dry martinis, died in 2011. In 1983, my old friend Alfred Friendly shot himself in an upstairs bedroom at the age of seventy-one, having sent his wife to a party, saying he didn't feel up to it. He was in the advanced stages of cancer of the throat and lung.

My younger brothers are both dead. David's death was just awful. It was when I was at the Ministry of Agriculture, so over twenty years ago now. David had been ill – with what, I never quite knew, but it was something to do with his balance. He had been to the States to try to get treatment but was now back in Milan, seeing another specialist. One day at work David was meeting another J. Walter Thomson director. The chap was in his office on the telephone and said, 'Just a minute.' David went out to wait in the corridor and fell down the stairwell, four storeys, onto a marble floor. He fell on his head and died instantly. Margaret Thatcher wrote me a letter to say how sorry she was, which was very touching. My other brother, Alastair, died last year.

Robin Carey-Evans, my first boyfriend, is still alive, and living in Australia. We write to each other, but he doesn't come over any more, which – although perhaps understandable at our great age – is a shame, as I remain very fond of him. I believe the American is still alive: I talked to him on the telephone about two years ago and it was the same old voice, but we've not been in touch since then. Ronnie Furse is still alive too, a widower now, living in America. I remember with great sadness the night poor Ronnie's wife Pam died. My dear old friend from New York days had settled back in England with Pam, where they had both become enthusiastic cattle farmers. One morning I took a hysterical phone call from Ronnie. He had woken up to find Pam lying in bed beside him, dead. He was in tears, so I quickly said, 'I'm on my way,' and put the phone down. I was a minister at the time so always had a car and a chauffeur at my disposal. We drove like mad straight down to Sussex. Grief and shock does funny things to people's voices and I remember that when we arrived Ronnie was speaking in a high falsetto, still in floods of tears. It was terrible.

No one died when my flat caught fire in 2010, thankfully, but it certainly felt like a bereavement. It happened on a freezing cold January night. I had been out playing bridge and when my taxi dropped me off at my flat in Battersea at about 11.30, there were fire engines everywhere, and the entire mansion block had been barred off by the police. I paid my taxi driver and went over to one of the policemen, asking, in a happy go lucky sort of way,

'I live here, can I possibly go along and get in?' He asked me what number and I told him. 'Come with me,' he said. It was a dreadful, dreadful shock. The fire had started in my bedroom with something electrical and had only been spotted when a man passing by noticed the flames pouring out into the garden. It was my bed which had been merrily burning away and had blown the windows out.

My daughter-in-law came and drove me down to their house in Sussex. She was so kind, and so warm, but I remember going into their spare room and almost screaming with misery. I felt so lonely. I had nothing. No clothes, nothing.

Everything in my bedroom was burnt, and the smoke damage was incredible. I lost so many things: beautiful things, valuable things, meaningful things. I lost almost everything from my childhood, including a lovely comfy Edwardian nanny chair that I had carefully carted from house to house my entire life. (Perhaps because my mother used to give away my dearest things every time we moved house, I am a terrible hoarder.) I lost a carpet I had lovingly stitched over three solid years, with squares to represent all the things I loved the most: horses, dogs, Staffordshire china. That carpet was my pride and joy. I lost tables and chairs I had bought from the antique shops on Eton High Street, my father's racing cups and all my old recipes. Of the few things I have left, some of my most treasured possessions are those that have been given to me by old friends and colleagues – like a beautiful screen from Ronnie and a carriage clock from Folkestone Racecourse.

But something funny always seems to happen to me. And the funny thing this time was that after the insurance people took everything away to assess the damage, they returned anything that hadn't been ruined, including some of my clothes. A lot of the clothes they returned, though, weren't actually mine, but they fitted me. So I kept them. The shoes didn't fit, nor the hats, but some of the clothes most certainly did, which was rather marvellous.

*

There are still some lovely holidays: until a couple of years ago, when travel became too difficult, my great friends Lord and Lady Arran used to invite me to their house in the South of France every summer. It was three weeks of pure bliss. We relaxed by the pool all day and in the evenings we ate our way around Provence. We went to a different restaurant every night, talent scouting for Tommy. He was looking for really good French chefs who he could persuade to come and cook for him at his shooting parties in Devon.

And there are still a few parties. I threw one myself for my ninetieth birthday. I held it in the House of Lords, and invited 300 people – a contingent from every part of my life, which I thought was rather lovely. My hairdresser came, and the ladies who help me with my shopping at Waitrose, and the policemen who are so kind to me at the House of Lords, and so on.

John Major made a lovely and very funny speech. I had first got to know John when he, Edwina Currie and I had all been ministers in the Department of Health. I never had a clue what was going on between them. Later, when John was prime minister and I was a government whip, I asked him after a couple of weeks how it was going. He said, 'It's simply ghastly. I have Margaret ringing me up every day and telling me what to do.' She couldn't give it up. Especially to him. I got to know John very well and am terribly fond of him and of Norma. I think he was much more canny than they gave him credit for at the time.

David Cameron couldn't be there but he wrote me a letter. Lord Strathclyde, who was then our Leader in the Lords, handed the letter to me, and I put it on the table, unread, because I was busy talking to everyone. When I went back to collect it, it was gone. Someone had taken the letter. Can you imagine? And I had never read it. It was awful, but I had to confess to him, and he wrote me another. I hadn't meant him to do it, but I thought it was jolly decent of him.

It was a wonderful party, but the curious thing was, none of them drank the champagne. I had imported cases and cases of champagne from France but they all drank white wine.

CHAPTER FOURTEEN

Still Having Fun

Unsurprisingly, perhaps, having celebrated my ninetieth birthday, and attended the funerals of so many of my dear friends, I've got my own memorial service all planned out. In fact, I did it years ago. It will be in St Margaret's, Westminster, the beautiful sixteenth-century church that stands between the Houses of Parliament and Westminster Abbey. Everyone will sing 'All Things Bright and Beautiful', to represent my love of animals and the countryside, and the fact that I was an agriculture minister, and the 'Battle Hymn of the Republic', to represent my love of America. Cambridge City Council will fly the town hall flag at half mast as they do for every ex-mayor. Lord Elton and Lord Deben will speak. They were both absolutely terrific bosses when I was a minister and have remained dear dear friends. Then I will be cremated. I am not a religious person at all, I am afraid; I believe we are as flowers in the field: we grow, we die and that is it.

Being quite so old is a frightful bore. My eyes are very bad these days, and I was very unwell in the summer of 2013. I lost so much weight my rings kept falling off and then I couldn't see to find them again. Being slimmer is rather a novelty, but the rest is a nuisance. However, I don't want to strike a glum note, because I am never glum. Instead, I plan to just keep on going, and keep on having as much fun as I can.

I don't sit on committees any more, and I make fewer contributions than I used to now that I am no longer a minister, but I still go to the House of Lords every day that it is sitting, if I possibly can. And, though it still terrifies me, I still stand up and speak on occasion, if the subject for debate is something I feel strongly about, or one where I think my experience is particularly helpful. It's a great mistake to speak up on a subject about which you know nothing. That is true generally, but especially in the Lords. The other day I nearly got up to speak about obesity and chocolates. I was going to make a joke at my own expense. But something stopped me and I was rather glad it did. However, after some encouragement from my friend Lord Elton, I did recently get up to ask a minister 'whether he agrees that this particular Question is a damned silly one'. I loved saying 'damned silly' – it's such a good phrase – and I got a big laugh.

On a more serious note, I am always keen to contribute

on anything to do with Bletchley Park and secret war work. Most recently I have continued to campaign hard on behalf of Alan Turing. And I do hope that my contribution, as someone who was at Bletchley, will have carried some weight. Given the recent royal pardon, I think it might have done. When the pardon was announced, in December, I rang up Downing Street to leave a message for the prime minister. The person who answered the phone told me, 'Oh, we don't take telephone messages, you've got to write a letter.' And I said, 'No, I'm not going to write a letter. And you take the following message and please see that it gets there. My name is Lady Trumpington and I wish to say, "Lady Trumpington wishes to thank the Prime Minister with regard to Turing."' And that's all.' 'Yes, I will,' he said. I do hope he did. I think it's marvellous that Turing's name has been cleared after all these years.

But apart from the Lords, since my appearance on *Have I Got News for You* I seem to have been asked to do a lot of television, and I've found I rather enjoy it. Recently, I took part in a documentary about older women who like clothes, called *Fabulous Fashionistas*. There were six of us on it, all seventy or eighty or ninety. I was the oldest. One was a model, one bought all her clothes at charity shops, one was a dancer and choreographer, one was a woman who used to have a cookery programme in the 1980s and one had got a job at Gap after her husband died. I didn't know any of them before the programme and we had nothing in common really except that we all love clothes, and we all love life, and none of us give a damn what other people think about us. Since the programme people have been tweeting about me, I gather, which I don't really understand, and there was a private viewing in King's Cross attended by all manner of wild and wonderful people. Adam took the six of us, plus the director, for lunch at the Turf Club which was quite an occasion. And the choreographer, Gillian Lynne, invited me to see *Phantom of the Opera*, which is one of her shows. I arrived at the theatre on Haymarket and was taken by the doorman in a wheelchair up to the Royal Box. Just before the curtain went up, the doorman appeared again and wheeled me back down, and across Haymarket to another theatre. He and his fellow doorman, happily for me, must have been talking because I had turned up at the wrong place. I wonder what I would have seen if I had stayed there.

Then that charming young man, Jack Whitehall, invited me onto his talk show, *Backchat*, just before Christmas, which was enormously jolly. I was on there with Nigel Havers, which made all my friends die with envy although I didn't like his beard, and the comedian Lee Mack. Lee was put on as kind of a foil for Jack, I think, but he spent most of his time looking after me –

and very kind he was too. The Olympic athlete Kriss Akabusi was also on the programme, handing out Christmas presents to all of us dressed up as 'Santabusi'. I liked him very much; he was a great giggler.

In the same week, I was asked to be a judge on a Second World War-themed episode of the *Great British Menu*. The food was delicious, but making the programme was exhausting. I was there from seven in the morning until ten at night. Every two hours or so the three professional judges would disappear from the studio. I had no idea what they were doing but afterwards I found out that they were ringing up their friends and writing letters. Nobody suggested I might like to have a break so I just went on sitting in the green room, but they might have thought of something for me to do. At one stage I'd got so bored I went out to talk to the cooks, one of whom gave me a goody bag of the leftovers of his dish to take home. When you see the programme on the television it looks as though they're cooking in huge kitchens but in fact they're tiny, not much bigger than my kitchen in Battersea.

I've loved horses and racing since I was a child and both still give me immense pleasure. On my ninety-first birthday, my good friend Selina Boyce gave me the most wonderful treat. Adam drove me to Newmarket and Selina organized lunch at the Jockey Club and we visited two studs there. We went to see their top stallion, Frankel, and I was allowed to give him Polo Mints out of my hand; it was such a thrill, it really was. The first time I saw Frankel race, years ago now at Ascot, it was just incredible. I think he won by about twenty lengths. He was right up at the front by himself while the other horses were miles behind. He ran fourteen races in all and he was never beaten. That's quite something. And it goes to show, too, because I was brought up never to pick a horse with a white ankle: it was supposed to be unlucky. And yet Frankel has four of them. Four little white socks. Now his pregnant wives are selling for four-and-a-half million pounds. Each. People are very hopeful for those foals but I don't think it will work. After all, Frankel's father was a good boy and he won some good races but he wasn't anything to scream about.

*

So here I am, still going in my ninety-second year, still enjoying life as much as I always have. I am so terribly lucky to have been sustained throughout these latter years of my life by the kindness of my friends, my hairdresser Bobby, my taxi driver, my two ladies at Waitrose, the very very many people at the House of Lords and, of course, most of all, by my son Adam. Thanks to them, I still have the most wonderful life, and I still behave rather badly and I still have such fun.

extracts reading groups

competitions books new

discounts extracts extracts

competitions discounts events

books new extracts reading groups

reading groups events books

new books extracts discounts

new reading groups

interviews extracts

reading groups books events new reading groups

events extracts extracts books

discounts events interviews new books extracts

new books events events

events new events

discounts extracts discounts books

www.panmacmillan.com

extracts events reading groups

competitions books extracts new